TRUE

SUBMISSION

THE CHARLES G. FINNEY MEMORIAL LIBRARY

Evangelistic Sermon Series
- So Great Salvation
- The Guilt of Sin
- True and False Repentance
- God's Love for a Sinning World

Revival Sermon Series
- Victory Over the World
- True Saints
- True Submission

Sermons on Prayer
- Prevailing Prayer

TRUE SUBMISSION

Revival Messages

CHARLES G. FINNEY

KREGEL PUBLICATIONS
GRAND RAPIDS, MICHIGAN 49501

First Printing............................1967
Reprinted...............1975, 1979, 1982, 1985

Library of Congress Catalog Card Number 66-24881
ISBN 0-8254-2618-9

This series of sermons selected from
Lectures to Professing Christians and *The Way of Salvation*
by Charles G. Finney

Printed in the United States of America

CONTENTS

PUBLISHER'S FOREWORD

Why this new edition of the sermons of Charles Grandison Finney? Because in many ways the days in which we are living are a duplicate of the day and situation in which Finney himself proclaimed the message which God had given him — the call to evangelism and to revival. These messages speak to our day in no uncertain sound for conditions within the church, and in the world around, call for a voice from God, a resounding clarion call for return to the Biblical standard of Christian life, and the God-ordained plan of redemption and revival.

These have been chosen and arranged with the needs of the world and church today in view. They are as applicable in this day of falling away and departure from the faith as they were in Finney's day. Heart-searching and uncompromising, they cut away the froth and frills so apparent in much modern preaching to reveal God's message for a sinning world, a world seemingly intent upon self-destruction and self-aggrandizement.

It is the publisher's prayer that these messages in their new form will convey God's message to our needy world, revealing His will and purpose for His Church — and His divine plan of salvation for an unbelieving generation.

The Publishers

1

TRUE CHARACTER

"Examine yourselves, whether ye be in the faith; prove your own selves." 2 Cor. 13:5.

IN speaking from this text I design to pursue the following order:

I. Show what is intended by the requirement in the text.

II. The necessity of this requirement.

III. The practicability of the duty enjoined.

IV. Give some directions as to the manner of performing the duty.

I. I am to show what is intended by the requirement in the text, "Examine yourselves, whether ye be in the faith; prove your own selves."

It requires that we should understand our own hearts, that we should take the proper steps to make proof of our real characters, as they appear in the sight of God. It refers not to a trial of proof of our strength, or knowledge, but our moral character, that we should thoroughly test it, so as to understand it as it is. It implies that we should know how God regards us, and what he thinks of us—whether he considers us saints or sinners. It is nothing less than a positive command that we should ascertain our own true character, and settle the question definitely for ourselves, whether we are saints or sinners, heirs of heaven or heirs of hell.

II. I am to show the necessity of this requirement.

1. It is indispensable to our own peace of mind, that we should prove and ascertain our true character, as it is in the sight of God.

The individual who is uncertain as to his real character, can have no such thing as settled peace of mind. He may have apathy more or less complete and perfect, but apathy is very different from peace. And very few professors of religion, or persons who continue to hear the gospel, can have such apathy for any length of time, as to suppress all uneasy feelings, at being uncertain respecting their true character and destiny. I am not speaking of hypocrites, who have seared their consciences, or of scoffers who may be given up of God. But in regard to others, it is strictly true that they must have this question settled in order to enjoy peace of mind.

2. It is essential to christian honesty.

A man who is not truly settled in his mind as to his own character is hardly honest in religion. If he makes a profession of religion when he does not honestly believe himself a saint, who does not know that that is not exactly honest? He is half a hypocrite at heart. So when he prays, he is always in doubt whether his prayers are acceptable, as coming from a child of God.

3. A just knowledge of one's own character is indispensable to usefulness.

If a person has always to agitate this question in his mind, "Am I a Christian?"—if he has to be always anxiously looking at his own estate all the while, and doubtful how he stands, it must be a great hindrance to his usefulness. If when he speaks to sinners, he is uncertain whether he is not himself a sinner, he cannot exhort with that confidence and simplicity, that he could if he felt his own feet on a rock. It is a favorite idea with some people, that it is best for saints to be always in the dark, to keep them humble. Just as if it was calculated to make a child of God proud to know that he is a child of God. Whereas, one of the most weighty considerations in the universe to keep him from dishonoring God is, to know that he is a child of God. When a person is in an anxious state of mind, he can have but little faith, and his usefulness cannot be extensive till the question is settled.

III. The practicability of this requirement.

It is a favorite idea with some, that in this world the question never can be settled. It is amazing what a number of persons there are, that seem to make a virtue of their great doubts, which they always have, whether they are Christians. For hundreds of years it has been looked upon by many as a suspicious circumstance, if a professor of religion is not filled with doubts. It is considered as almost a certain sign, he knows nothing of his own heart. One of the universal questions put to candidates for admission has been, "Have you any doubts of your good estate?" And if the candidate answers, "O yes, I have great doubts," that is all very well, and is taken as evidence that he is spiritual, and has a deep acquaintance with his own heart, and has a great deal of humility. But if he has no doubts, it is taken as evidence that he knows little of his own heart, and is most probably a hypocrite. Over against all this, I maintain that the duty enjoined in the text is a practicable duty, and that Christians can put themselves to such a proof, as to know their own selves, and have a satisfactory assurance of their real character.

1. This is evident from the command in the text, "Examine yourselves, whether ye be in the faith; prove your own selves." Will any one believe that God requires us to examine ourselves and prove ourselves, and see what is our true character, when he knows it to be impossible for us ever to learn our true character.

2. We have the best possible medium of proof, to try ourselves and prove our character, and that is our consciousness.

Consciousness gives the highest possible certainty as to the facts by which our characters are to be determined, and the great question is settled. What is our state before God? We may have, and ought to have, the same kind of evidence of our state before God as we have of our existence; and that is, consciousness. Nay, we cannot help having the evidence. Consciousness is continually testifying what are our states of mind, and it only needs for us to take notice of what consciousness testifies, and we can settle the question as certainly as we can our own existence.

3. God gives men such constant opportunities to act out what is in their hearts, that nothing but negligence can prevent their coming to a decision of the matter.

If men, were shut up in dungeons, where they had no opportunity to act, and no chance of being influenced by circumstances, and no way to develop the state of their hearts, they would not be so much to blame for not knowing themselves. But God has placed them in the circumstances in which they are in this life on purpose, as he said to the children of Israel, to prove them, and to know what is in their hearts, and whether they will keep his commandments or no. The things around us must produce an impression on our minds, and lead us to feel and act in some way. And this affords opportunities of self-knowledge, when we see how we feel and how we are inclined to act in such diversified circumstances.

4. We are farther qualified to trust to our own true characters, by having a perfect rule to try them by.

The law of God is a true standard by which to try our characters. We know exactly what that is, and we have therefore an infallible and an invariable rule by which to judge of ourselves. We can bring our feelings and actions to this rule, and compare them with this standard, and know exactly what is their true character in the sight of God, for God himself tries them by the same standard.

5. Our circumstances are such that nothing but dishonesty can possibly lead us to self-deception.

The individual who is self-deceived is not only careless and negligent, but decidedly dishonest, or he would not deceive himself. He must be to a great degree prejudiced by pride, and blinded by self-will or he could not but know that he is not what he professes to be. The circumstances are so many and so various, that call forth the exercises of his mind, that it must be wilful blindness that is deceived. If they never had any opportunities to act, or if circumstances did not call forth their feelings, they might be ignorant. A person who had never seen a beggar, might not be able to tell what were his true feelings towards beggars. But place him where he meets beggars every day, and he must be wilfully blind or dishonest, if he do not know the temper of his heart towards a beggar.

IV. I will mention a few things as to the manner of performing this duty.

First—Negatively.

1. It is not done by waiting for evidence to come to us.

Many seem to wait, in a passive attitude, for the evidence to come to them, to decide whether they are Christians or not. They appear to have been waiting for certain feelings to come to them. Perhaps they pray about it; perhaps they pray very earnestly, and then wait for the feelings to come which will afford them satisfactory evidence of their good estate. Many times they will not do anything in religion till they get this evidence, and they sit and wait, and wait, in vain expectation that the Spirit of God will come some time or other, and lift them out of this slough, while they remain thus passive and stupid. They may wait till doomsday and never get it in this way

2. Not by any direct attempt to force the feelings into exercise which are to afford the evidence.

The human mind is so constituted, that it never will feel by trying to feel. You may try as hard as you please, to feel in a particular way. Your efforts to put forth feel-

ings are totally unphilosophical and absurd.   There is now
nothing before the mind to produce emotion or feeling.
Feeling is always awakened in the mind by the mind's being intensely fixed on some object calculated to awaken
feeling.   But when the mind is fixed, not upon the object,
but on direct attempts to put forth feeling, this will not
awaken feeling.   It is impossible.   The attention must be
taken up with the object calculated to awaken feeling, or
there will be no feeling.   You may as well shut up your
eyes and attempt to see, or go into a dark room.   In a dark
room there is no object to awaken the sense of sight and
you may *exert* yourself and strain your eyes, and try to see,
but you will see nothing.   When the mind's attention is
taken up with looking inward, and attempting to examine
the nature of the present emotion, that emotion at once
ceases to exist, because the attention is no longer fixed on
the object that causes the emotion.   I hold my hand before this lamp, it casts a shadow ; but if I take the lamp
away, there is no shadow ; there must be a light to produce a shadow.   It is just as certain that if the mind is
turned away from the object that awakens emotion, the
emotion ceases to exist.   The mind must be fixed on the
object, not on the emotion, or there will be no emotion,
and consequently no evidence.

3. You will never get evidence by spending time in
mourning over the state of your heart.

Some people spend their time in nothing but complaining, " O, I don't feel, I can't feel, my heart is so hard."
What are they doing ?   Nothing but mourning and crying
because they don't feel.   Perhaps they are trying to work
themselves up into feeling !   Just as philosophical as trying to fly.   While they are mourning all the while, and
thinking about their hard hearts, and doing nothing, they
are the ridicule of the devil.   Suppose a man should shut
himself out from the fire and then go about complaining

how cold he is, the very children would laugh at him.   He must expect to freeze, if he will shut himself out from the means of warmth.   And all his mournings and feeling bad will not help the matter.

Second—Positively.   What must be done in this duty ?

If you wish to test the true state of your heart with regard to any object, you must fix your attention on that object.   If you wish to test the power or accuracy of sight, you must apply the faculty to the object, and then you will test the power and state of that faculty.   You place yourself in the midst of objects, to test the state of your eyes ; or in the midst of sounds, if you wish to test the perfectness of your ears.   And the more you shut out other objects that excite the other senses, and the more strongly you fasten your minds on this one, the more perfectly you test the keenness of your vision, or the perfectness of your hearing.   A multiplicity of objects is liable to distract the mind.   When we attend to any object calculated to awaken feeling, it is impossible not to feel.   The mind is so constituted that it cannot but feel.   It is not necessary to stop and ask, " Do I feel ? "   Suppose you put your hand near the fire, do you need to stop and ask the question, " Do I really feel the sensation of warmth ? "   You know, of course, that you do feel.   If you pass your hand rapidly by the lamp, the sensation may be so slight as not to be noticed, but is none the less real, and if you paid attention strictly enough, you would know it.   Where the impression is slight, it requires an effort of attention to notice your own consciousness.   So the passing feeling of the mind may be so slight as not to occupy your thoughts, and thus may escape your notice, but it is not the less real.   But hold your hand in the lamp a minute, and the feeling will force itself upon your notice, whatever be your other occupations.   If the mind is fixed on an object calculated to excite emotions of any kind, it is impossible not to feel those emotions in a degree ; and if the mind is intently fixed, it is impossible not to feel the emotions in such a degree as to be conscious that they exist.   These principles will show you how we are to come at the proof of our characters, and know the real state of our feelings towards any object.   It is by fixing our attention on the object till our emotions are so excited that we become conscious what they are.

I will specify another thing that ought to be borne in mind.   Be sure the things on which your mind is fixed, and on which you wish to test the state of your heart are realities.

There is a great deal of imaginary religion in the world, which the people who are the subjects of it mistake for real.   They have high feelings, their minds are much excited, and the feeling corresponds with the object contemplated.   But here is the source of the delusion—the object is imaginary.   It is not that the feeling is false or imaginary.   It is real feeling.   It is not that the feeling does not correspond with the object before the mind.   It corresponds perfectly.   But the object is a fiction.   The individual has formed a notion of God, or of Jesus Christ, or of salvation, that is altogether aside from the truth, and his feelings in view of these imaginations are such as they would be towards the true objects, if he had true religion, and so he is deluded.   Here is undoubtedly a great source of the false hope and professions in the world.

V. I will now specify a few things on which it is your duty to try the state of your minds.

1. Sin—not your own particular sins, but sin itself, as an outrage committed against God.

You need not suppose you will get at the true state of your hearts merely, by finding in your mind a strong feeling of disapprobation of sin.   This belongs to the nature of an intelligent being, as such.   All intelligent beings feel a disapprobation of sin, when viewed abstractedly, and without reference to their own selfish gratification. The devil, no doubt, feels it. The devil no more feels approbation for sin, when viewed abstractly, than Gabriel. He blames sinners and condemns their conduct, and whenever he has no selfish reason for being pleased at what they do, he abhors it. You will often find in the wicked on earth, a strong abhorrence of sin. There is not a wicked man on earth, that would not condemn and abhor sin, in the abstract. The mind is so constituted, that sin is universally and naturally and necessarily abhorrent to right reason and to conscience. Every power of the mind revolts at sin. Man has pleasure in them that commit iniquity, only when he has some selfish reason for wishing them to commit it. No rational being approves of sin, as sin.

But there is a striking difference between the constitutional disapprobation of sin, as an abstract thing, and that hearty detestation and opposition that is founded on love to God. To illustrate this idea. It is one thing for that youth to feel that a certain act is wrong, and quite another thing to view it as an injury to his father. Here is something in addition to his former feeling. He has not only indignation against the act as wrong, but his love to his father produces a feeling of *grief* that is peculiar. So the individual who loves God feels not only a strong disapprobation of sin, as wrong, but a feeling of grief mingled with indignation when he views it as committed against God.

If, then, you want to know how you feel towards sin,—how do you feel when you move around among sinners, and see them break God's law? When you hear them swear profanely, or see them break the Sabbath, or get drunk, how do you feel? Do you feel as the Psalmist did when he wrote, "I beheld the transgressors, and was grieved, because they kept not thy word?" So he says, "Rivers of waters run down mine eyes, because they keep not thy law." And again, " Horror hath taken hold upon me, because of the wicked that forsake thy law."

2. You ought to test the state of your hearts towards your own sins.

Look back on your past sins, call up your conduct in former times, and see whether you do cordially condemn it and loathe it, and feel as an affectionate child would feel, when he remembers how he has disobeyed a beloved parent. It is one thing to feel a strong conviction that your former conduct was wicked. It is quite another thing to have this feeling attended with strong emotions of grief, because it was sin against God. Probably there are few Christians who have not looked back upon their former conduct towards their parents with deep emotion, and thought how a beloved father and an affectionate mother have been disobeyed and wronged ; and who have not felt, in addition to a strong disapprobation of their conduct, a deep emotion of grief, that inclined to vent itself in weeping, and perhaps did gush forth in irrepressible tears. Now this is true repentance towards a parent. And repentance towards God is the same thing, and if genuine, it will correspond in degree to the intensity of attention with which the mind is fixed on the subject.

3. You want to test your feelings towards impenitent sinners.

Then go among them, and converse with them, on the suoject of their souls, warn them, see what they say, and how they feel, and get at the real state of their hearts, and then you will know how you feel towards the impenitent. Do not shut yourself up in your closet and try to imagine an impenitent sinner. You may bring up a picture of the imagination that will affect your sympathies, and make you weep and pray. But go and bring your heart in contact with the living reality of a sinner, reason with him, exhort him, find out his cavils, his obstinacy, his insincerity, pray with him if you can. You cannot do this without waking up emotions in your mind, and if you are a Christian, it will wake up such mingled emotions of grief, compassion and indignation, as Jesus Christ feels, and as will leave you no room to doubt what is the state of your heart on this subject. Bring your mind in contact with sinners, and fix it there, and rely on it you will feel.

4. You want to prove the state of your mind towards God.

Fix your thoughts intently on God. And do not set yourselves down to imagine a God after your own foolish hearts, but take the Bible and learn there what is the true idea of God. Do not fancy a shape or appearance, or imagine how he looks, but fix your mind on the Bible description of how he feels and what he does, and what he says, and you cannot but feel. Here you will detect the real state of your heart. Nay, this will constitute the real state of your heart, which you cannot mistake.

5. Test your feelings towards Christ.

You are bound to know whether you love the Lord Jesus Christ or not. Run over the circumstances of his life, and see whether they appear as realities to your mind, his miracles, his sufferings, his lovely character, his death, his resurrection, his ascension, his intercession now at the right hand of the throne of God. Do you believe all these? Are they realities to your mind? What are your feelings in view of them? When you think of his willingness to save, his ability to save, his atoning death, his power, if these things are realities to you, you will have feelings of which you will be conscious, and concerning which there will be no mistake.

6. What are your feelings towards the saints.

If you wish to test your heart on this point, whether you love the saints, do not let your thoughts run to the ends of the earth, but fix your mind on the saints by you

and see whether you love them, whether you desire their
sanctification, whether you really long to have them grow
in grace, whether you can bear them in your heart to the
throne of grace in faith, and ask God to bestow blessings
on them.

7. So in regard to revivals.

You wish to know what is the state of your feelings towards revivals, then read about them, think of them, fix
your mind on them, and you cannot but have feelings tha
will evince the state of your heart. The same is true of
the heathen, of the slaves, of drunkards, of the Bible, of
any object of pious regard. The only way to know the
state of your heart is to fix your mind on the reality of
those things, till you feel so intensely that there is no mis-
taking the nature of your feelings.

Should you find a difficulty in attending to any of
these objects sufficiently to produce feeling, it is owing to
one of two reasons, either your mind is taken up with
some other parts of religion, so as not to allow of such
fixed attention to the specified object, or your thoughts
wander with the fool's eyes, to the ends of the earth. The
former is sometimes the case, and I have known some
Christians to be very much distressed because they did not
feel so intensely as they think they ought, on some subjects.
Their own sins, for instance. A person's mind may be so
much taken up with anxiety, and labor, and prayer for
sinners, that it requires an effort to think enough about
his own soul to feel deeply, and when he goes on his knees
to pray about his own sins, that sinner with whom he has
been talking comes right up before his mind and he can
hardly pray for himself. It is not to be regarded as evidence against you, if the reason why you do not feel on
one subject in religion is because your feelings are so en-
grossed about another, of equal importance. But if your
thoughts run all over the world, and that is the reason

you do not feel deeply enough to know what is your true character, if your mind will not come down to the Bible, and fix on any object of religious feeling, lay a strong hand on yourself, and fix your thoughts with a death-grasp, till you do feel. You can command your thoughts : God has put the control of your mind in your own hands. And in this way, you can control your own feelings, by turning your attention upon the object you wish to feel about. Bring yourself, then, powerfully and resolutely, to that point, and give it not over till you fasten your mind to the subject, and till the deep fountains of feeling break up in your mind, and you know what is the state of your heart, and understand your real character in the sight of God.

CONCLUSION

1. Activity in religion is indispensable to self-examination.

An individual can never know what is the true state of his heart, unless he is active in the duties of religion. Shut up in his closet, he never can tell how he feels towards objects that are without, and he never can feel right towards them until he goes out and acts. How can he know his real feeling towards sinners, if he never brings his mind in contact with sinners ? He goes into his closet, and his imagination may make him feel, but it is a deceitful feeling, because not produced by a reality. If you wish to test the reality of your feelings towards sinners, go out and warn sinners, and then the reality of your feelings will manifest itself.

2. Unless persons try their hearts by the reality of things, they are constantly subject to delusion, and are all the time managing to delude themselves.

Suppose an individual shut up in a cloister, shut out from the world of reality, and living in a world of imagination. He becomes a perfect creature of imagination. So

it is in religion, with those who do not bring their **mind**
in contact with realities. Such persons think they love
mankind, and yet do them no good. They imagine they
abhor sin, and yet do nothing to destroy it. How many
persons deceive themselves, by an excitement of the imagination about missions, for instance ; how common it **is**
for persons to get up a great deal of feeling, and hold
prayer meetings for missions, who really do nothing to
save souls. Women will spend a whole day at a prayer
meeting to pray for the conversion of the world, while
their impenitent servant in the kitchen is not spoken to
all day, and perhaps not in a month, to save her soul.
People will get up a public meeting, and talk about feeling
for the heathen, when they are making no direct efforts
for sinners around them. This is all a fiction of the imagination. There is no reality in such a religion as that.
If they had real love of God, and love of souls, and **real**
piety, the pictures drawn by the imagination about **the**
distant heathen would not create so much more **feeling**
than the reality around them.

It will not do to say, it is because their attention is **not**
turned towards sinners around them. They hear the pro-
fane oaths, and see the Sabbath-breaking and other vices,
as a naked reality before their eyes, every day. And if
these produce no feeling, it is in vain to pretend that they
feel as God requires for sinners in heathen lands, or anywhere. Nay, take this very individual, now so full of
feeling for the heathen, as he imagines, and place him
among the heathen—transport him to the Friendly Islands,
or elsewhere, away from the fictions of imagination, and
in the midst of the cold and naked reality of heathenism,
and all his deep feeling is gone. He may write letters
home about the abominations of the heathen, and all that,
but his feeling about their salvation is gone. You hear
people talk so about the heathen, who have never converted

a soul at home—rely upon it, that is all imagination. If they do not promote revivals at home, where they understand the language and have direct access to their neighbors, much less can they be depended on to promote the real work of religion on heathen ground. The churches ought to understand this, and keep it in mind in selecting men to go on foreign missions. They ought to know that if the naked reality at home does not excite a person to action, the devil would only laugh at a million such missionaries.

The same delusion often manifests itself in regard to revivals. There is an individual who is a great friend to revivals. But mark—they are always revivals of former days, or of revivals in the abstract, or distant revivals, or revivals that are yet to come. But as to any present revival, he is always found aloof and doubtful. He can read about revivals in President Edwards' day, or in Scotland, or in Wales, and be greatly excited and delighted. He can pray, " O Lord, revive thy work ; O, Lord, let us have such revivals, let us have a pentecost season, when thousands shall be converted in a day." But get him into the reality of things, and he never happens to see a revival in which he can take any interest, or feel real complacency. He is friendly to the fictitious imaginings of his own mind ; he can create a state of things that will excite his feelings, but no naked reality ever brings him out to coöperate in actually promoting a revival.

In the days of our Saviour, the people said, and no doubt really believed, that they abhorred the doings of those who persecuted the prophets. They said, " If we had been in the days of our fathers, we would not have been partakers with them of the blood of the prophets." No doubt they wondered that people could be so wicked as to do such things. But they had never seen a prophet ; they were moved simply by their imagination. And as soon as the Lord Jesus Christ appeared, the greatest of prophets, on whom all the prophecies centred, they rejected him, and finally put him to death, with as much cold-hearted cruelty as ever their fathers had killed a prophet. "Fill ye up," says our Saviour, " the measure of your fathers, that upon you may come all the righteous blood shed upon the earth."

Mankind have always, in every age of the world, fallen in love with the fictions of their own imagination, over which they have stumbled into hell. Look at the Universalist. He imagines a God that will save everybody, at any rate, and a heaven that will accommodate everybody ; and then he loves the god he has made, and the heaven he has imagined, and perhaps will even weep with love. His feelings are often deep, but they are delusive, because excited by fiction and not by truth.

3. The more an individual goes out from himself, and makes things not belonging to himself the subject of thought, the more piety he will have, and the more evidence of his piety.

Religion consists in love, in feeling right and doing right, or doing good. If therefore you wish to have great piety, do not think of having it by cultivating it in a way which never caused piety to grow ; that is, by retiring into a cloister, and withdrawing from contact with mankind. If the Lord Jesus Christ had supposed such circumstances to be favorable to piety, he would have directed them so. But he knew better. He has therefore appointed circumstances as they are, so that his people may have a thousand objects of benevolence, a thousand opportunities to do good. And if they go out of themselves, and turn their hearts upon these things, they cannot fail to grow in piety, and to have their evidences increasing and satisfactory.

4. It is only in one department of self-examination that

we can consistently shut ourselves up in the closet to perform the duty ; that is, when we want to look back and calmly examine the motives of our past conduct. In such cases it is often necessary to abstract our thoughts and keep out other things from our minds, to turn our minds back and look at things we have done, and the motives by which we were actuated. To do this effectually, it is often necessary to resort to retirement, and fasting, and prayer. Sometimes it is impossible to wake up a lively recollection of what we wish to examine, without calling in the laws of association to our aid. We attempt to call up past scenes, and all seems confusion and darkness, until we strike upon some associated idea, that gradually brings the whole fresh before us. Suppose I am to be called as a witness in court concerning a transaction, I can sometimes gain a lively recollection of what took place, only by going to the place, and then all the circumstances come up, as if but of yesterday. So we may find in regard to the reëxamination of some part of our past history, that no shutting ourselves up will bring it back, no protracted meditation or fasting, or prayer, till we throw ourselves into some circumstances that will wake up the associated ideas, and thus bring back the feelings we formerly had.

Suppose a minister wishes to look back and see how he felt, and the spirit with which he had preached years ago. He wishes to know how much real piety there was in his labors. He might get at a great deal in his closet on his knees, by the aid of the strong influences of the Spirit of God. But he will come at it much more effectually by going to the place, and preaching again there. The exact attitude in which his mind was before, may thus recur to him, and stand in strong reality before his mind.

5. In examining yourselves, be careful to avoid expecting to find all the graces of the Christian in exercise in your mind at once.

This is contrary to the nature of mind. You ought to satisfy yourselves, if you find the exercises of your mind are right, on the subject that is before your mind. If you have wrong feelings at the time, that is another thing. But if you find that the emotions at the time are right, do not draw a wrong inference, because some other right emotion is not in present exercise. The mind is so constituted, that it can only have one train of emotions at a time.

6. From this subject you see why people often do not feel more than they do.

They are taking a course not calculated to produce feeling. They feel, but not on the right subjects. Mankind always feel on some subjects ; and the reason why they do not feel deeply on religious subjects is, because their attention is not deeply fixed on such subjects.

7. You see the reason why there is such a strange diversity in the exercises of real Christians.

There are some Christians whose feelings, when they have any feeling are always of the happy kind. There are others whose feelings are always of a sad and distressing kind. They are in almost constant agony for sinners. The reason is, that their thoughts are directed to different objects. One class are always thinking of the class of objects calculated to make them happy ; the other are thinking of the state of the church, or the state of sinners, and weighed down as with a burden, as if a mountain were on their shoulders. Both may be religious, both classes of feelings are right, in view of the objects at which they look. The apostle Paul had continual heaviness and sorrow of heart on account of his brethren. No doubt he felt right. The case of his brethren, who had, rejected the Saviour, was so much the object of his thoughts, the dreadful wrath that they had brought upon themselves, the doom that hung over them, was constantly before his mind, and how could he be otherwise than sad ?

8. Observe the influence of these two classes of feelings in the usefulness of individuals.

Show me a very joyful and happy Christian, and he is not generally a very useful Christian. Generally, such are so taken up with enjoying the sweets of religion, that they do but little. You find a class of ministers, who preach a great deal on these subjects, and make their pious hearers very happy in religion, but such ministers are seldom instrumental in converting many sinners, however much they may have refreshed, and edified, and gratified saints. On the other hand you will find men who are habitually filled with deep agony of soul in view of the state of sinners, and these men will be largely instrumental in converting men. The reason is plain. Both preached the truth, both preached the gospel, in different proportions, and the feelings awakened correspond with the views they preached. The difference is, that one comforted the saints the other converted sinners.

You may see a class of professors of religion who are always happy, and they are lovely companions, but they are very seldom engaged in pulling sinners out of the fire. You find others always full of agony for sinners, looking at their state, and longing to have souls converted. Instead of enjoying the antepast of heaven on earth, they are sympathizing with the Son of God when he was on earth, groaning in his spirit, and spending all night in prayer.

9. The real revival spirit is a spirit of agonizing desires and prayer for sinners.

10. You see how you may account for your own feelings at different times.

People often wonder why they feel as they do. The answer is plain. You feel so, because you think so. You direct your attention to those objects which are calculated to produce those feelings.

11. You see why some people's feelings are so changeable.

There are many whose feelings are always variable and unsteady. That is because their thoughts are unsteady. If they would fix their thoughts, they would regulate their feelings.

12. You see the way to beget any desired state of feeling in your own mind, and how to beget any desired state of feeling in others.

Place the thoughts on the subject that is calculated to produce those feelings, and confine them there, and the feelings will not fail to follow.

13. There are multitudes of pious persons who dishonor religion by their doubts.

They are pepetually talking about their doubts, and they take up a hasty conviction that they have no religion. Whereas if instead of dwelling on their doubts they will fix their minds on other subjects, on Christ for instance, or go out and seek sinners, and try to bring them to repentance, rely upon it, they will feel, and feel right, and feel so as to dissipate their doubts.

Remember, you are not to wait till you feel right before you do this. Perhaps some things that I said to this church have not been rightly understood. I said you could do nothing for God unless you felt right. Do not therefore infer, that you are to sit still and do nothing till you are satisfied that you do feel right. But place yourself in circumstances to make you feel right, and go to work. On one hand, to bustle about without any feeling is no way, and on the other hand, to shut yourself up in your closet and wait for feeling to come, is no way. Be sure to be always active. You never will feel right otherwise. And then keep your mind constantly under the influence of those objects that are calculated to create and keep alive Christian feelings.

2

SELFISHNESS

"Seeketh not her own."   1 Cor. 13:5.

THAT is, Charity, or Christian love, seeketh not her own.

The proposition which I design to establish this evening, is the following :

That a supreme regard to our own happiness is inconsistent with true religion.

This proposition is naturally the first in the series that I have been laboring to illustrate in the present lectures, and would have been the first to be discussed, had I been aware that it was seriously called in question by any considerable number of professed Christians.   But I can honestly say, that when I commenced these lectures, I did not expect to meet any serious difficulty here ; and therefore I took it in a great measure for granted, that selfishness is not religion.   And hence, I passed over this point with but a slight attempt at proving it.   But since, I learn that there are many professed Christians who maintain that a supreme regard to our own happiness is true religion, I think it nesessary to examine the subject more carefully, and give you the arguments in favor of what I suppose to be the truth.   In establishing my proposition, I wish to distinguish between things that differ ; I shall therefore,

I. Show what is not intended by the proposition, that a supreme regard to our own happiness is not religion.

II. Show what is meant by it.

III. Attempt to prove it.

I. I am to explain what is not meant by the proposition.

1. The point in dispute is not, whether it is lawful to

have any regard to our own happiness. On the contrary, it is admitted and maintained to be a part of our duty to have a due regard to our own happiness, according to its real value, in the scale with other interests. God has commanded us to love our neighbor as ourselves. This plainly makes it a duty to love ourselves or regard our own happiness, by the same rule that we regard that of others.

2. The proposition is not that we ought to have no regard to the promises and threatenings of God, as affecting ourselves. It is plainly right to regard the promises of God and threatenings of evil, as affecting ourselves, according to the relative value of our own interests. But who does not see that a threatening against us is not so important as a threatening against a large number of individuals. Suppose a threatening of evil against yourself as an individual. This is plainly not so important as if it included your family. Then suppose it extends to the whole congregation, or to the state, or the whole nation, or the world. Here, it is easy to see, that the happiness of an individual, although great, ought not to be regarded as supreme.

I am a minister. Suppose God says to me, " If you do not do your duty, you shall be sent to hell." This is a great evil, and I ought to avoid it. But suppose him to say, " If your people do not do their duty, they will all be sent to hell ; but if you do your duty faithfully, you will probably save the whole congregation." Is it right for me to be as much influenced by the fear of evil to myself, as by the fear of having a whole congregation sent to hell ? Plainly not.

3. The question is not whether our own eternal internal interests ought to be pursued in preference to our temporal interests. It is expressly maintained by myself, and so it is by the Bible, that we are bound to regard our eternal interests as altogether of more consequence than our temporal interests.

Thus the Bible tells us " Labor not for the meat that perisheth, but for that which endureth unto everlasting life." This teaches that we are not to regard or value our temporal interests at all, in comparison with eternal life.

So, where our Saviour says, " Lay not up for yourselves treasures on the earth, where moth and rust doth corrupt, and where thieves break through and steal ; but lay up for yourselves treasures in heaven, where neither moth nor rust doth corrupt, and where thieves break not through nor steal." Here the same duty is enjoined, of preferring eternal to temporal interests.

There is another. When Christ sent out his disciples, two and two, to preach and to work miracles, they came back full of joy and exultation, because they found even the devils yielding to their power. " Lord, even the devils are subject to us." Jesus saith, " Rejoice not that the devils are subject to you ; but rather rejoice in this, that your names are written in heaven." Here he teaches, that it is a greater good to have our names written in heaven, than to enjoy the greatest temporal power, even authority over devils themselves.

The Bible everywhere teaches, that eternal good is to be preferred in all our conduct to temporal good. But this is very different from maintaining that our own individual eternal interest is to be aimed at as the supreme object of regard.

4. The proposition is not, that hope and fear should not influence our conduct. All that is implied is, that when we are influenced by hope and fear, the things that are hoped or feared should be put into the scale according to their real value, in comparison with other interests.

5. The question is not, whether the persons did right, who are spoken of in the Bible, as having been at least in some degree influenced by hope and fear, or having respect unto the recompense of reward, or to the joy that was set

before them. This is admitted. Noah was moved with
fear and built the ark. But was it the fear of being
drowned himself, or fear for his own personal safety that
chiefly moved him ? The Bible does not say it. He feared
for the safety of his family ; yea, more, he dreaded the de-
struction of the whole human race, with all the interests
depending thereon.

Whenever it is said that good men were influenced by
hope and fear, it is admitted. But in order to make it
bear on this subject, it must be shown that this hope or
fear respecting their own personal interest was the controlling motive. Now, this is no where affirmed in the Bible.
It was right for them to be influenced by promises and
threatenings. Otherwise they could not obey the second
part of the law: " Thou shalt love thy neighbor as thyself."

II. I am to show what is meant by the proposition, that
supreme regard to our own interest is inconsistent with
true religion.

The question is, whether supreme regard to our own
happiness is religion. It is, whether we are to fear our
own damnation more than the damnation of all other men,
and the dishonor of God thereby. And whether we are to
aim at securing our own happiness more than the happiness of all other men, and the glory of God. And whether,
if we do this, we act according to the requirements of the
true religion, or inconsistent with true religion. This is the
proper point of inquiry, and I wish you to bear it constantly
in mind, and not to confound it with any of the other
points that I have referred to.

III. For the proof of the proposition.

Before proceeding to the proof of the proposition, that
a supreme regard to our own happiness is inconsistent with
true religion, I will observe that all true religion consists
in being like God ; in acting on the same principles and
grounds, and having the same feelings towards different

objects. I suppose this will not be denied. Indeed, it cannot be, by any sane mind. I then observe, as the first proof of the proposition,

1. That a supreme regard to our own happiness is not according to the example of God ; but is being totally unlike him.

The Bible tells us that "God is love." That is, benevolence is the sum total of his character. All his other moral attributes, such as justice, mercy, and the like, are but modifications of his benevolence. His love is manifested in two forms. One is that of benevolence, good willing, or desiring the happiness of others. The other complacency, or approving the character of others who are holy. God's benevolence regards all beings that are capable of happiness. This is universal. Towards all holy beings, he exercises the love of complacency. In other words, God loves his neighbor as himself. He regards the interests of all beings, according to their relative value, as much as his own. He seeks his own happiness, or glory, as the supreme good. But not because it is his own, but because it is the supreme good. The sum total of his happiness, as an infinite being, is infinitely greater than the sum total of the happiness of all other beings, or of any possible number of finite creatures.

Take a very familiar illustration. Here is a man that is kind to brutes. This man and his horse fall into the river. Now, does true benevolence require the man to drown himself in order to extricate his horse ? No. It would be true disinterested benevolence in him, to save himself, and, if need be, leave his horse to perish ; because his happiness is of so much greater value than that of the horse. You see this at a glance. But the difference between God and all created beings is infinitely greater than between a man and a horse, or between the highest angel and the meanest insect.

God, therefore, regards the happiness of all creatures precisely according to its real value. And unless we do the same we are not like God. If we are like God, we must regard God's happiness and glory in the same light that he does ; that is, as the supreme good, beyond every thing else in the universe. And if we desire our own happiness more than God's happiness, we are infinitely unlike God.

2. To aim at our own happiness supremely is inconsistent with true religion, because it is contrary to the spirit of Christ.

We are told, that "if any man have not the spirit of Christ, he is none of his." And it is repeatedly said of him, as a man, that he sought not his own, that he sought not his own glory, and the like. What was he seeking ? Was it his own personal salvation ? No. Was it his own personal happiness ? No. It was the glory of his Father, and the good of the universe, through the salvation of men. He came on an errand of pure benevolence, to benefit the kingdom of God, not to benefit himself. This was " the joy that was set before him," for which " he endured the cross, despising the shame." It was the great good he could do by thus throwing himself out to labor and suffer for the salvation of men.

3. To regard our own happiness as the supreme object of pursuit is contrary to the law of God.

I have mentioned this before, but recur to it again for the sake of making my present demonstration complete. The sum of that law is this—" Thou shalt love the Lord thy God, with all thy heart, and with all thy soul, and with all thy mind, and with all thy strength ; and thou shalt love thy neighbor as thyself." This is the great thing required ; benevolence towards God and man. The first thing is really to love the happiness and glory of God, above all other things, because it is so infinitely lovely and desira

ble, and is properly the supreme good. Some have ob-
jected that it was not our duty to seek the happiness of God,
because his happiness is already secured. Suppose, now,
that the king of England is perfectly independent of me,
and has his happiness secured without me ; does that make
it any the less my duty to wish him well, to desire his happiness, and to rejoice in it ? Because God is happy, in
himself, independent of his creatures, is that a reason why
we should not love his happiness, and rejoice in it ?
Strange.

Again : We are bound by the terms of God's law to exercise complacency to God, because he is holy, infinitely
holy.

Again : This law binds us to exercise the same good
will, or benevolence, towards others that we do to ourselves;
that is, to seek both their interests and our own, according
to their relative value. Who of you is doing this ? And
we are bound to exercise the love of complacency towards
those who are good and holy.

Thus we see that the sum of the law of God is to exercise benevolence towards God and all beings, according to
their relative value, and complacency in all that are holy.
Now I say that to regard our own happiness supremely, or
to seek it as our supreme end, is contrary to **that law, to**
its letter and to its spirit. And,

4. It is as contrary to the gospel as it is to the law.

In the chapter from which the text is taken, the apostle begins—" Though I speak with the tongues of men and
of angels, and have not charity, I am become as sounding
brass, or a tinkling cymbal. And though I have the gift
of prophecy, and understand all mysteries and all knowledge ; and though I have all faith, so that I could remove
mountains, and have not charity, I am nothing." Charity
here means love. In the original it is the same word that
is rendered love. " And though I bestow all my goods to

feed the poor, and though I give my body to be burned, and have not charity, it profiteth me nothing."

Now mark! In no stronger language could he have expressed the idea that charity, or benevolence, is essential to true religion. See how he throws out his guards on every side, so that it is impossible to mistake his views. If a person has not true charity, he is nothing. He then proceeds and shows what are the characteristics of this true charity. "Charity suffereth long, and is kind; charity envieth not; charity vaunteth not itself, is not puffed up, doth not behave itself unseemly, seeketh not her own, is not easily provoked, thinketh no evil; rejoiceth not in iniquity, but rejoiceth in the truth; beareth all things, believeth all things, hopeth all things, endureth all things." Here you see that one leading peculiarity of this love is, that charity "seeketh not her own." Mark that. If this is true religion, and without it there is no religion, then one peculiarity of true religion is, that it "seeketh not her own."

Those of you who have Bibles with marginal references can follow out these references and find a multitude of passages that plainly teach the same thing. Recollect the passages I quoted in the last lecture. I will just refer to one of them—"Whosoever will save his life shall lose it." Here you see it laid down as an established principle of God's government, that if a person aims supremely at his own interest he will lose his own interest.

The same is taught in the tenth chapter of this epistle, verse 24: "Let no man seek his own, but every man another's wealth." If you look at the passage, you will see that word "wealth" is in italic letters, to show that it is a word added by the translators, that is not in the Greek. They might just as well have used the word happiness, or welfare, as wealth. So in the 33d verse: "Even as I please all men in all things, *not seeking my own profit*, but the profit of many, that they may be saved."

Therefore I say, that to make our own interest the **su-preme** object of pursuit, is as contrary to the gospel as it is to the law.

5. It is contrary to conscience.

The universal conscience of mankind has decided that a supreme regard to our own happiness is not virtue. Men have always known that to serve God and benefit mankind is what is right, and to seek supremely their own personal interest is not right. They have always regarded it mean and contemptible for individuals to seek their own happiness as the supreme object, and consequently, we see how much pains men take to conceal their selfishness and to appear benevolent. It is impossible for any man, unless his conscience is strangely blunted by sin, or perverted by false instruction, not to see that it is sinful to regard his own happiness above other interests of more importance.

6. It is contrary to right reason.

Right reason teaches us to regard all things according to their real value. God does this, and we should do the same. God has given us reason for this very purpose, that we should weigh and compare the relative value of things. It is a mockery of reason, to deny that it teaches us to regard things according to their real value. And if so, then to aim at and prefer our own interest, as the supreme end, is contrary to reason.

7. It is contrary to common sense.

What has the common sense of mankind decided on this point? Look at the common sense of mankind in regard to what is called patriotism. No man was ever regarded as a true patriot, in fighting for his country, if his object was to subserve his own interest. Suppose it should appear that his object in fighting was to get himself crowned king; would anybody give him credit for patriotism? No. All men agree that it is patriotism when a man is disinterested, like Washington; and fights for his country, for his country's sake. The common sense of mankind has written reprobation on that spirit that seeks its own things, and prefers its own interest, to the greater interests of others. It is evident that all men so regard it. Otherwise, how is it that every one is anxious to appear disinterested.

8. It is contrary to the constitution of the mind.

I do not mean, by this, that it is impossible, by our very constitution, for us to seek our own happiness as the supreme object. But we are so constituted that if we do this, we never can attain it. As I have said in a former lecture, happiness is the gratification of desire. We must desire something, and gain the object we desire. Now, suppose a man to desire his own happiness, the object of his desire will always keep just so far before him, like his shadow, and the faster he pursues it the faster it flies. Happiness is inseparably attached to the attainment of the object desired. Suppose I desire a thousand dollars. That is the thing on which my desire fastens, and when I get it that desire is gratified, and I am happy, so far as gratifying this desire goes to make me happy. But if I desire the thousand dollars for the purpose of getting a watch, a dress, and such like things, the desire is not gratified till I get those things. But now suppose the thing I desired was my own happiness. Getting the thousand dollars then does not make me happy, because that is not the thing my desire was fixed on. And so getting the watch, and dress, and other things, do not make me happy, for they gratify not my desire. God has so constituted things, and given such laws to the mind, that man never can gain happiness by pursuing it. This very constitution plainly indicates the duty of disinterested benevolence. Indeed, he has made it impossible for them to be happy, but in proportion as they are disinterested.

Here are two men walking along the street together.

They come across a man that has just been run over by a
cart, and lies weltering in his gore. They take him up,
and carry him to the surgeon, and relieve him. Now it is
plain that their gratification is in proportion to the intensity of their desire for his relief. If one of them felt but
little and cared but little about the sufferings of the poor
man, he will be but little gratified. But if his desire to
have the man relieved amounted to agony, his gratification
would be accordingly. Now suppose a third individual
that had no desire to relieve the distressed man ; certainly
relieving him could be no gratification to that person.
He could pass right by him, and see him die. Then he is
not gratified at all. Therefore you see, happiness is just
in proportion as the desires are gratified by obtaining the
things desired.

Here observe, that in order to make the happiness of
gratified desire complete, the desire itself must be virtuous. Otherwise, if the desire is selfish, the gratification
will be mingled with pain, from the conflict of the mind.

That all this is true, is a matter of consciousness, and
is proved to us by the very highest kind of testimony we
can have. And for any one to deny it, is to charge God
foolishly, as if he had given us a constitution that would
not allow us to be happy in obeying him.

9. It is also inconsistent with our own happiness, to make
our own interest the supreme object. This follows from
what I have just said. Men may enjoy a certain kind of
pleasure, but not true happiness. The pleasure which
does not spring from the gratification of virtuous desire,
is a deceptive delusion. The reason why all mankind do
not find happiness, when they are all so anxious for it, is
that they are seeking *it*. If they would seek the glory of
God, and the good of the universe as their supreme end,
it would pursue them.

10. It is inconsistent with the public happiness. If

each individual is to aim at his own happiness as his chief end, these interests will unavoidably clash and come into collision, and universal war and confusion will follow in the train of universal selfishness.

11. To maintain that a supreme regard to our own interest is true religion, is to contradict the experience of all real saints. I aver, that every real saint knows that his supreme happiness consists in going out of himself, and regarding the glory of God and the good of others. If he does not know this he is no saint.

12. It is also inconsistent with the experience of all those who have had a selfish religion, and have found out their mistake and got true religion. This is a common occurrence. I suppose I have known hundreds of cases. Some members in this church have recently made this discovery ; and they can all testify that they now know, by experience, that benevolence is true religion.

13. It is contrary to the experience of all the impenitent. Every impenitent sinner knows that he is aiming supremely at the promotion of his own interest, and knows that he has not true religion. The very thing that his conscience condemns him for is this, that he is regarding his own interest instead of the glory of God.

Now just turn the leaf over, for a moment, and admit that a supreme regard for our own happiness is true religion ; and then see what will follow.

1. Then it will follow that God is not holy. That is, if a supreme regard to our own interest, because it is our own, is true religion, then it will follow that God is not holy. God regards his own happiness, but it is because it is the greatest good, not because it is his own. But he is love, or benevolence ; and if benevolence is not true religion, God's nature must be changed.

2. The law of God must be altered. If a supreme regard to our own happiness is religion, then the law should

read, "Thou shalt love thyself with all thy heart and with all thy soul, and with all thy mind, and with all thy strength, and God and thy neighbor infinitely less than thyself."

3. The gospel must be reversed. Instead of saying "Whether ye eat or drink, or whatsoever ye do, do all to the glory of God, it should read, "Do all for your own happiness." Instead of "He that will save his life shall lose it," we should find it saying, "He that is supremely anxious to save his own life shall save it ; but he that is benevolent, and willing to lose his life for the good of others, shall lose it."

4. The consciences of men should be changed so as to testify in favor of selfishness, and condemn and reprobate every thing like disinterested benevolence.

5. Right reason must be made not to weigh things according to their relative value, but to decide our own little interest to be of more value than the greatest interests of God and the universe.

6. Common sense will have to decide, that true patriotism consists in every man's seeking his own interest instead of the public good, and each one seeking to build himself up as high as he can.

7. The human constitution must be reversed. If supreme selfishness is virtue, the human constitution was made wrong. It is so made, that man can be happy only by being benevolent. And if this doctrine is true, that religion consists in seeking our own happiness as a supreme good, then the more religion a man has the more miserable he is.

8. And the whole frame-work of society will have to be changed. Now it is so, that the good of the community depends on the extent to which every one regards the public interest. And if this doctrine holds, it must be changed, so that the public good will be best promoted

when every man is scrambling for his own interest regardless of the interests of others.

9. The experience of the saints will have to be reversed. Instead of finding, as they now do, that the more benevolence they have, the more religion and the more happiness, they should testify that the more they aim at their own good, the more they enjoy of religion and the favor of God.

10. The impenitent should be found to testify that they are supremely happy in supreme selfishness, and that they find true happiness in it.

I will not pursue this proof any farther ; it would look like trifling. If there is any such thing as proof to be had, it is fully proved, that to aim at our own happiness supremely, is inconsistant with true religion.

CONCLUSION

1. We see why it is, that while all are pursuing happiness, so few find it.

The fact is plain. The reason is this ; the greater part of mankind do not know in what true happiness consists. and they are seeking it in that which can never afford it. They do not find it because they are pursuing it. If they would turn round and pursue holiness, happiness would pursue them. If they would become disinterested, and lay themselves out to do good, they could not but be happy. If they choose happiness as an end, it flies before them. True happiness consists in the gratification of virtuous desires ; and if they would set themselves to glorify God, and do good, they would find it. The only class of persons that never do find it, in this world, or the world to come, are those who seek it as an end.

II. The constitution of the human mind and of the universe, affords a beautiful illustration of the economy of God.

Suppose man could find happiness, only by pursuing

his own happiness.   Then each individual would have only the happiness that himself had gained, and all the happiness in the universe would be only the sum total of what individuals had gained, with the offset of all the pain and misery produced by conflicting interests.   Now mark! God has so constituted things, that while each lays himself out to promote the happiness of others, his own happiness is secured and made complete.   How vastly greater then is the amount of happiness in the universe, than it would have been, had selfishness been the law of Jehovah's kingdom.   Because each one who obeys the law of God, fully secures his own happiness by his benevolence, and the happiness of the whole is increased by how much each receives from all others.

Many say, "Who will take care of my happiness if I do not? If I am to care only for my neighbor's interest, and neglect my own, none of us will be happy."   That would be true, if your care for your neighbor's happiness were a detraction from your own.   But if your happiness consists in doing good and promoting the happiness of others, the more you do for others, the more you promote your own happiness.

III. When I gave out the subject of this lecture, I avoided the use of the term, selfishness, lest it should be thought invidious.   But I now affirm, that a supreme regard to our own interest is selfishness, and nothing else. It would be selfishness in God, if he regarded his own interest supremely because it is his own.   And it is selfishness in man.   And whoever maintains that a supreme regard to our own interest is true religion, maintains that selfishness is true religion.

IV. If selfishness is virtue, then benevolence is sin. They are direct opposites and cannot both be virtue.   For a man to set up his own interest over God's interest, giving it a preference, and placing it in opposition to God's inter-

est is selfishness And if this is virtue, then Jesus Christ,
in seeking the good of mankind as he did, departed from
the principles of virtue. Who will pretend this ?

V. Those who regard their own interest as supreme,
and yet think they have true religion, are deceived. I say
it solemnly, because I believe it is true, and I would say it
if it were the last word I was to speak before going to the
judgment. Dear hearer, whoever you are, if you are doing this, you are not a Christian. Don't call this being
censorious. I am not censorious. I would not denounce
any one. But as God is true, and your soul is going to
the judgment, you have not the religion of the Bible.

VI. Some will ask here, "What ! are we to have no
regard to our happiness, and if so, how are we to decide
whether it is supreme or not ? " I do not say that. I say,
you may regard it according to its relative value. And now
I ask, is there any real practical difficulty here ? I appeal
to your consciouness. You cannot but know, if you are
honest, what it is that you regard supremely. Are these
interests, your own interest on one side, and God's glory
and the good of the universe on the other, so nearly bal-
anced in your mind, that you cannot tell which you prefer ? It is impossible ! If you are not as conscious that
you prefer the glory of God to your own interest, as you
are that you exist, you may take it for granted that you are
all wrong.

VII. You see why the enjoyment of so many professors
of religion depends on their evidences. These persons are
all the time hunting after evidence ; and just in proportion
as that varies, their enjoyments wax and wane. Now,
mark ! If they really regarded the glory of God and the
good of mankind, their enjoyment would not depend on
their evidences. Those who are purely selfish, may enjoy
much in religion, but it is by anticipation. The idea of
going to heaven is pleasing to them. But those who go

out of themselves, and are purely benevolent, have a present heaven in their breasts.

VIII. You see, here, that all of you who had no peace and joy in religion before you had a hope, are deceived. Perhaps I can give an outline of your experience. You were awakened, and were distressed, as you had reason to be, by the fear of going to hell. By and by, perhaps while you were engaged in prayer, or while some person was conversing with you, your distress left you. You thought your sins were pardoned. A gleam of joy shot through your mind, and warmed up your heart into a glow, that you took for evidence, and this again increased your joy. How very different is the experience of a true Christian ! His peace does not depend on his hope ; but true submission and benevolence produce peace and joy, independent of his hope.

Suppose the case of a man in prison, condemned to be hung the next day. He is in great distress, walking his cell, and waiting for the day. By and by, a messenger comes with a pardon. He seizes the paper, turns it up to the dim light that comes through his grate, reads the word *pardon*, and almost faints with emotion, and leaps for joy. He supposes the paper to be genuine. Now suppose it turns out that the paper is counterfeit. Suddenly his joy is all gone. So in the case of a deceived person. He was afraid of going to hell, and of course he rejoices if he believes he is pardoned. If the devil should tell him so, and he believed it, his joy would be just as great, while the belief lasts, as if it was a reality. True Christian joy does not depend on evidence. He submits himself into the hands of God with such confidence, and that very act gives him peace. He had a terrible conflict with God, but all at once he yields the controversy, and says, " God will do right, let God's will be done." Then he begins to pray, he is subdued, he melts down before God, and that very act af-

fords sweet, calm, and heavenly joy. Perhaps he has **not**
thought of a hope. Perhaps he may go for hours, or even
for a day or two, full of joy in God, without thinking of
his own salvation. You ask him if he has a hope, he never
thought of that. His joy does not depend on believing that
he is pardoned, but consists in a state of mind, acquiescing
in the government of God. In such a state of mind, he
could not but be happy.

Now let me ask which religion have you? If you exercise true religion, suppose God should put you into hell,
and there let you exercise supreme love to God, and the
same love to your neighbor as to yourself, that itself is a
state of mind inconsistent with being miserable.

I wish this to be fully understood. These hope-seekers
will be always disappointed. If you run after hope, you
will never have a hope good for anything. But if you pursue
holiness, hope, and peace, and joy, will come of course.
Is your religion the love of holiness, the love of God and of
souls? Or is it only a hope?

IX. You see why it is that anxious sinners do not find
peace.

They are looking at their own guilt and danger. They
are regarding God as an avenger, and shrinking from his
terrors. This will render it impossible they should ever
come at peace. While looking at the wrath of God, making them wither and tremble, they cannot love him, they
hide from him. Anxious sinners, let me tell you a secret.
If you keep looking at that feature of God's character, it
will drive you to despair, and that is inconsistent with true
submission. You should look at his whole character, and
see the reasons why you should love him, and throw yourself upon him without reserve, and without distrust; and
instead of shrinking from him, come right to him, and
say, "O, Father in heaven, thou art not inexorable, thou
art sovereignty, but thou art good, I submit to thy govern-

ment, and give myself to thee, with all I have and all I am, body and soul, for time and for eternity."

3

TRUE SUBMISSION

"Submit yourselves therefore to God." James 4:7.

THE subject of this lecture is, "*What constitutes True Submission?*"

Before I enter on the discussion of this subject, I wish to make two remarks, introductory to the main question.

1. The first remark is this : If any of you are deceived in regard to your hopes, and have built on a false foundation, the fundamental error in your case was your embracing what you thought was the gospel plan of salvation from selfish motives. Your selfish hearts were unbroken This is the source of your delusion, if you are deceived. If your selfishness was subdued, you are not deceived in your hope. If it was not, all your religion is vain, and your hope is vain.

2. The other remark I wish to make is, that if any of you are deceived, and have a false hope, you are in the utmost danger of reviving your old hope, whenever you are awakened to consider your condition. It is a very common thing for such professors, after a season of anxiety and self-examination, to settle down again on the old foundation. The reason is, their habits of mind have become fixed in that channel, and therefore, by the laws of the mind it is difficult to break into a new course. It is indispensable, therefore, if you ever mean to get right, that you should see clearly that you have hitherto been wholly wrong, so that you need not multiply any more the kind of efforts that have deceived you heretofore.

Who does not know that there is a great deal of this kind of deception ? How often will a great part of the

50

church lie cold and dead, till a revival commences? Then you will see them bustling about, and they get engaged, as they call it, in religion, and renew their efforts and multiply their prayers for a season; and this is what they call getting revived. But it is only the same kind of religion that they had before. Such religion lasts no longer than the public excitement. As soon as the body of the church begin to diminish their efforts for the conversion of sinners, these individuals relapse into their former worldliness, and get as near to what they were before their supposed conversion, as their pride and their fear of the censures of the church will let them. When a revival comes again, they renew the same round; and so they live along by spasms, over and over again, revived and backsliden, revived and backsliden, alternately, as long as they live. The truth is, they were deluded at first, by a spurious conversion, in which selfishness never was broken down; and the more they multiply such kind of efforts, the more sure they are to be lost.

I will now enter upon the direct discussion of the subject, and endeavor to show you what true gospel submission is, in the following order, *viz*;

I. I shall show what is not true submission.

II. Show what true submission is.

I. I am to show what true submission is not.

1. True submission to God is not indifference. No two things can be more unlike than indifference and true submission.

2. It does not consist in being willing to be sinful for the glory of God. Some have supposed that true submission included the idea of being willing to be sinful for the glory of God. But this is a mistake. To be willing to be sinful is itself a sinful state of mind. And to be willing to do anything for the glory of God, is to choose not to be sinful. The idea of being sinful for the glory of God is absurd.

3. It does not consist in a willingness to be punished.

If we were now in hell, true submission would require that we should be willing to be punished. Because then it would be certain that it was God's will we should be punished. So, if we were in a world where no provision was made for the redemption of sinners, and where our punishment was therefore inevitable, it would be our duty to be willing to be punished. If a man has committed murder, and there is no other way to secure the public interest but for him to be hung, it is his duty to be willing to be hung for the public good. But if there was any other way in which the murderer could make the public interest whole, it would not be his duty to be willing to be hung. So if he were in a world solely under law, where there was no plan of salvation, and no measure to secure the stability of government in the forgivness of sinners, it would be the duty of every man to be willing to be punished. But as it is in this world, genuine submission does not imply a willingness to be punished. Because we know it is not the will of God that all shall be punished, but on the other hand, we know it is his will that all who truly repent and submit to God shall be saved.

II. I am to show what genuine submission is.

1. It consists in perfect acquiescence in all the providential dealings and dispensations of God ; whether relating to ourselves, or to others, or to the universe. Some persons suppose they do acquiesce in the abstract, in the providential government of God. But yet, if you converse with them you see they will find fault with God's arrangements in many things. They wonder why God suffered Adam to sin ? Or why he suffered sin to enter the universe at all ? Or why he did this or that ? Or why he made this or that, thus or so ? In all these cases, supposing we could assign no reason at all that would be satisfactory, true submission implies a perfect acquiescence in

whatever he has suffered or done ; and feeling that, so far as his providence is concerned, it is all right.

2. True submission implies acquiescence in the precept of God's moral law. The general precept of God's moral law is, "Thou shalt love the Lord thy God, with all thy heart, and with all thy mind, and with all thy soul, and with all thy strength, and thou shalt love thy neighbor as thyself." Perhaps some will say , "I do acquiesce in this precept, I feel that it is right, and I have no objection to this law." Here I want you to make the distinction carefully between a constitutional approbation of God's law, and actual submission to it. There is no mind but what naturally, and by its own common sense of what is right, approves of this law. There is not a devil in hell that does not approve of it. God has so constituted mind, that it is impossible to be a moral agent, and not approve of his law. But this is not the acquiescence I am speaking of. A person may feel this approbation to so great a degree as to be even delighted without having true submission to it. There are two ideas included in genuine submission, to which I wish your particular attention.

(1.) The first idea is, that true acquiescence in God's moral law includes actual obedience. It is vain for a child to pretend a real acquiescence in his father's commands, unless he actually obeys them. It is in vain for a citizen to pretend an acquiescence in the laws of the land, unless he obeys the laws.

(2.) The main idea of submission is the yielding up of that which constitutes the great point in controversy. And that is this; that men have taken off their supreme affection from God and his kingdom, and set up self-interest as the paramount object of regard. Instead of laying themselves out in doing good, as God requires, they have adopted the maxim that "Charity begins at home." This is the very point in debate, between God and the sinner. The sinner aims at promoting his own interest, as his supreme ob-ject. Now, the first idea implied in submission is the yielding up of this point. We must cease placing our own interest as supreme, and let the interests of God and his kingdom rise in our affections just as much above our own interests as their real value is greater. The man who does not do this is a rebel against God.

Suppose a civil ruler were to set himself to promote the general happiness of his nation ; and should enact laws wisely adapted to this end, and should embark all his own resources in this object ; and that he should then require every subject to do the same. Then suppose an individual should go and set up his own private interest in opposition to the general interest. He is a rebel against the govern-ment, and against all the interest which the government is set to promote. Then the first idea of submission, on the part of the rebel, is giving up that point, and falling in with the ruler and the obedient subjects in promoting the public good. Now the law of God absolutely requires that you should make your own happiness subordinate to the glory of God and the good of the universe. And until you do this, you are the enemy of God and the universe, and a child of hell.

And the gospel requires the same as the law. It is astonishing that many, within a few years, have main-tained that it is right for a man to aim directly at his own salvation, and make his own happiness the great object of pursuit. But it is plain that God's law is different from this, and requires every one to prize God's interest su-premely. And the gospel requires the same with the law. Otherwise, Jesus Christ is the minister of sin, and came into the world to take up arms against God's government.

It is easy to show, from the Bible, that the gospel re-quires disinterested benevolence, or love to God and love to man, the same as the law. The first passage I shall quote is this, "Seek first the kingdom of God and his righteousness." What does that mean ? Strange as it may seem, a writer has lately quoted this very text to prove that it is right to seek first our own salvation, or our own happiness, and to make that the leading object of pursuit. But that is not the meaning. It requires every one to make the promotion of the kingdom of God his great object. I suppose it to enjoin the duty of aiming at being holy, and not at our own happiness. Happiness is connected with holiness, but it is not the same thing, but to seek holiness or obedience to God, and to honor and glorify him, is a very different thing from seeking supremely our own happiness.

Another passage is, "Whether ye eat or drink, or whatsoever ye do, do all to the glory of God." Indeed ! What! may we not eat and drink to please ourselves ? No. We may not even gratify our natural appetite for food, but as subordinate to the glory of God. This is what the gospel requires, for the apostle wrote this to the Christian church.

Another passage is, "Look not on your own things, but every man on the things of another." But it is vain to attempt to quote all the passages that teach this. You may find, on almost every page of the Bible, some passage that means the same thing, requiring us not to seek our own good, but the benefit of others.

Our Saviour says, "Whosoever will save his life shall lose it : and whosoever will lose his life shall save it." That is, If a man aim at his own interest, he shall lose his own interest ; if he aim at saving his soul, as his supreme object, he will lose his own soul ; he must go out of himself, and make the good of others his supreme object, or he will be lost.

And again he says, "There is no man that hath left house, or brethren, or sisters, or father, or mother, or wife, or children, or lands, for my sake and the gospel's, but he shall receive a hundred-fold now in this time, houses, and brethren, and sisters, and mothers, and children, and lands, with persecutions ; and in the world to come, eternal life." Here some people may stumble, and say, There is a reward held out as a motive. But, mark ! What are you to do ? Forsake self for the sake of a reward to self ? No ; but to forsake self for the sake of Christ and his gospel ; and the *consequence* will be as stated. Here is the important distinction.

In the 13th chapter of Corinthians Paul gives a full description of this disinterested love, or charity, without which a person is nothing in religion. It is remarkable how much he says a person may do, and yet be nothing. " Though I speak with the tongues of men and of angels, and have not charity, I am become as sounding brass, or a tinkling cymbal. And though I have the gift of prophecy and understand all mysteries, and all knowledge ; and though I have all faith, so that I could remove mountains, and have not charity, I am nothing. And though I bestow all my goods to feed the poor, and though I give my body to be burned, and have not charity, it profiteth me nothing." But true gospel benevolence is of this character : " Charity suffereth long and is kind ; charity envieth not; charity vaunteth not itself, is not puffed up, doth not behave itself unseemly, seeketh not her own, is not easily provoked, thinketh no evil ; rejoiceth not in iniquity, but rejoiceth in the truth ; beareth all things, believeth all things, hopeth all things, endureth all things." " Seeketh not her own." Mark that. It has no selfish end, but seeks the happiness of others as its great end. Without this kind of benevolence, we know there is not a particle of religion. You see, I might stand here all night quoting and explaining passages to the same point, showing that all pure religion consists in disinterested benevolence.

Before I go farther, I wish to mention several objections to this view, which may arise in your minds. I do this more particularly because some of you may stumble right here, and after all get the idea that it is right to have our religion consist in aiming at our own salvation as our great object.

Objection 1. "Why are the threatenings of the word of God given, if it is selfishness to be influenced by a fear of the wrath to come?"

Many answers may be given to this objection.

Answer. Man is so constituted that by the laws of his being he dreads pain. The Scripture threatenings, therefore, answer many purposes. One is, to arrest the attention of the selfish mind, and lead it to examine the reasons there are for loving and obeying God. When the Holy Spirit thus gets the attention, then he rouses the sinner's conscience, and engages that to consider and decide on the reasonableness and duty of submitting to God.

Objection 2. "Since God has given us these susceptibilities to pleasure and pain, is it wrong to be influenced by them?"

Answer. It is neither right nor wrong. These susceptibilities have no moral character. If I had time tonight, I might make all plain to you. In morals, there is a class of actions that come under the denomination of prudential considerations. For instance: Suppose you stand on a precipice, where, if you throw yourself down, you will infallibly break your neck. You are warned against it. Now, if you do not regard the warning, but throw yourself down, and destroy your life, that will be sin. But regarding it is no virtue. It is simply a prudential act. There is no virtue in avoiding danger, although it may often be sinful not to avoid it. It is sinful for men to brave the wrath of God. But to be afraid of hell is not holy, no more than the fear of breaking your neck down a precipice is holy. It is simply a dictate of the constitution.

Objection 3. "Does not the Bible make it our immediate duty to seek our own happiness ?"

Answer. It is not sinful to seek our own happiness, according to its real value. On the contrary, it is a real duty to do so. And he that neglects to do this, commits sin. Another answer is, that although it is right to seek our own happiness, and the constitutional laws of the mind require us to regard our own happiness, still our constitution does not indicate that to pursue our own happiness as the chief good, is right. Suppose any one should argue, that because our constitution requires food, therefore it is right to seek food as the supreme good—would that be sound ? Certainly not ; for the Bible expressly forbids any such thing, and says—" Whether ye eat or drink, do all to the glory of God."

Objection 4. " Each one's happiness is put particularly in his own power ; and if every one should seek his own happiness, the happiness of the whole will be secured, to the greatest amount that is possible."

This objection is specious, but not sound. I deny the conclusion altogether. For,

(1.) The laws of the mind are such, that it is impossible for one to be happy while he makes his own happiness the supreme object. Happiness consists in the gratification of virtuous desires. But to be gratified, the thing must be obtained "that is desired." To be happy, therefore, the desires that are gratified must be right, and therefore they must be disinterested desires. If your desires terminate on yourself ; for instance—if you desire the conversion of sinners for the sake of promoting your own happiness, when sinners are converted it does not make you happy, because it is not the thing on which your desire terminated. The law of the mind therefore, renders it impossible, if each individual pursues his own happiness, that he should ever obtain it. To be more definite. Two things are indispensable to true happiness. First, there must be virtuous desire. If the desire be not virtuous, conscience will remonstrate against it, and therefore a gratification would be attended with pain. Secondly, this desire must be gratified in the attainment of its object. The object must be desired for its own sake, or the gratification would not be complete, even should the object be obtained. If the object is desired as a means to an end, the gratification would depend on obtaining the end by this means. But if the thing was desired as an end, or for its own sake, obtaining it would produce unmingled gratification. The mind must, therefore, desire not its own happiness, for in this way it can never be attained, but the desire must terminate on some other object which is desired for its own sake, the attainment of which would be a gratification, and thus result in happiness.

(2.) If each one pursues his own happiness, as his supreme end, the interests of different individuals will clash, and destroy the happiness of all. This is the very thing we see in the world. This is the reason of all the fraud, and violence, and oppression, and wickedness in earth and hell. It is because each one is pursuing his own interest, and their interests clash. The true way to secure our own happiness is, not to pursue that as an end but to pursue another object, which, when obtained, will afford complete gratification—the glory of God and the good of the universe. The question is not, whether it is right to desire and pursue our own happiness at all, but whether it is right to make our own happiness our supreme end.

Objection 5. "Happiness consists in gratifying virtuous desire. Then the thing I aim at, is gratifying virtuous desire. Is not that aiming at my own happiness?"

Answer. The mind does not aim at gratifying the

desire, but at accomplishing the thing desired. **Suppose**
you see a beggar, as mentioned last week, and you give him
a loaf of bread. You aim at relieving the beggar. That
is the object desired, and when that is done, your desire is
gratified, and you are happy. But if, in relieving the
beggar, the object you aimed at was your own happiness,
then relieving the beggar will not gratify the desire, and
you render it impossible to gratify it.

Thus you see, that both the law and the gospel require
disinterested benevolence, as the only condition on which
man can be happy.

3. True submission implies acquiescence in the penalty
of God's law.

I again advert to the distinction, which I have made
before. We are not, in this world, simply under a government of naked law. This world is a province of Jehovah's
empire, that stands in a peculiar relation to God's government. It has rebelled, and a new and special provision has been made, by which God offers us mercy. The
conditions are, that we obey the precepts of the law, and
submit to the justice of the penalty. It is a government
of law, with the gospel appended to it. The gospel requires the same obedience with the law. It maintains
the ill desert of sin, and requires the sinner's acquiescence in the justice of the penalty. If the sinner were
under mere law, it would require that he should submit
to the infliction of the penalty. But man is not, and
never has been since the fall, under the government of
mere law, but has always known, more or less clearly, that
mercy is offered. It has, therefore, never been required,
that men should be willing to be punished. In this respect it is that gospel submission differs from legal submission. Under naked law, submission would consist in
willingness to be punished. In this world, submission
consists in acquiescence in the justice of the penalty, and

regarding himself as *deserving* the eternal wrath of
God.

4. True submission implies acquiescence in the sovereignty of God.

It is the duty of every sovereign to see that all his subjects submit to his government. And it is his duty to
enact such laws, that every individual, if he obeys perfectly, will promote the public good, in the highest possible
degree. And then, if any one refuses to obey, it is his
duty to take that individual by force, and make him subserve the public interest in the best way that is possible
with a rebellious subject, If he will not subserve the public good voluntarily he should be made to do it involun-
tarily. The government must either hang him, or shut
him up, or in some way make him an example of suffering ; or, if the public good admits of mercy, it may show
mercy in such a way as will best subserve the general interest. Now God is a sovereign ruler, and the submission
which he requires is just what he is bound to require.
He would be neglecting his duty as a ruler, if he did
not require it. And since you have refused to obey this requirement, you are now bound to throw yourself into his
hands, for him to dispose of you, for time and eternity,
in the way that will most promote the interests of the
universe. You have forfeited all claim to any portion
in the happiness of the universe or the favor of God.
And the thing which is now required of you is, that since
you cannot render obedience for the past, you should
acknowledge the justice of his law, and leave your future
destiny entirely and unconditionally at his disposal, for
time and for eternity. You must submit all you have
and all you are to him. You have justly forfeited all,
and are bound to give up all at his bidding, in any way
that he calls for them, to promote the interests of his
kingdom.

5. Finally, it requires submission to the terms of the gospel.   The terms of the gospel are—

(1.) Repentance, hearty sorrow for sin, justifying God and taking his part against yourself.

(2.) Faith, perfect trust and confidence towards God, such as leads you without hesitation to throw yourself, body and soul, and all you have and are, into his hand, to do with you as he thinks good.

(3.) Holiness, or disinterested benevolence.

(4.) To receive salvation as a mere matter of pure grace, to which you have no claim on the score of justice.

(5.) To receive Christ as your mediator and advocate, your atoning sacrifice, your ruler and teacher, and in all the offices in which he is presented to you in God's word. In short, you are to be wholly acquiescent in God's appointed way of salvation.

CONCLUSION

I. You see why there are so many false hopes in the church.

The reason is, that so many persons embrace what they consider the gospel, without yielding obedience to the law. They look at the law with dread, and regard the gospel as a scheme to get away from the law.   These tendencies have always been manifested among men.   There is a certain class that hold to the gospel and reject the law ; and another class that take the law and neglect the gospel. The Antinomians think to get rid of the law altogether. They suppose the gospel rule of life is different from the law ; whereas, the truth is, that the rule of life is the same in both, and both require disinterested benevolence. Now, if a person thinks that, under the gospel, he may give up the glory of God as his supreme object, and instead of loving God with all his heart, and soul, and strength, may make his own salvation his supreme object, his hopes

are false. He has embraced another gospel—which is no gospel at all.

II. The subject shows how we are to meet the common objection, that faith in Christ implies making our own salvation our object or motive.

Answer. What is faith ? It is not believing that *you* shall be saved, but believing God's word concerning his Son. It is no where revealed that you shall be saved. He has revealed the fact that Jesus Christ came into the world to save sinners. What you call faith, is more properly hope. The confident expectation that you shall be saved is an inference from the act of faith ; and an inference which you have a right to draw when you are conscious of obeying the law and believing the gospel. That is, when you exercise the feelings required in the law and gospel, you have a right to trust in Christ for your own salvation.

III. It is an error to suppose that despair of mercy is essential to true submission.

This is plain from the fact that, under the gospel, every body knows it is the will of God that every soul should be saved that will exercise disinterested benevolence. Suppose a man should come to me and ask, "What shall I do to be saved ?" and I should tell him, "If you expect to be saved you must despair of being saved," what would he think ? What inspired writer ever gave any such direction as this ? No, the inspired answer is, "Love the Lord thy God with all thy heart," "Repent," "Believe the Gospel," and so on. Is there any thing here that implies despair ?

It is true that sinners sometimes do despair, before they obtain true peace. But what is the reason ? It is not because despair is essential to true peace ; but because of their ignorance, or of wrong instructions given to them, or misapprehension of the truth. Many anxious sinners despair because they get a false impression that they have sinned away their day of grace, or that they have committed the unpardonable sin, or that their sins are peculiarly aggravated, and the gospel provision does not reach them. Sometimes they despair for this reason—they know that there is mercy provided, and ready to be bestowed as soon as they will comply with the terms, but they find all their efforts at true submission vain. They find they are so proud and obstinate, that they cannot get their own consent to the terms of salvation. Perhaps most individuals who do submit, do in fact come to a point where they give up all as lost. But is that necessary ? That is the question. Now, you see, it is nothing but their own wickedness drives them to despair. They are so unwilling to take hold of the mercy that is offered. Their despair, then, instead of being essential to true submission under the gospel, is inconsistent with it, and no man ever embraced the gospel while in that state. It is horrid unbelief, then, it is sin to despair ; and to say it is essential to true submission, is saying that sin is essential to true submission.

IV. True submission is acquiescing in the whole government of God.

It is acquiescing in his providential government, in his moral government, in the precept of his law, and in the penalty of his law, so that he is himself deserving of an exceeding great and eternal weight of damnation ; and submission to the terms of salvation in the gospel. Under the gospel, it is no man's duty to be willing to be damned. It is wholly inconsistent with his duty to be willing to be damned. The man who submits to the naked law, and consents to be damned, is as much in rebellion as ever ; for it is one of God's express requirements that he should obey the gospel.

V. To call on a sinner to be willing to be punished is a grand mistake, for several reasons.

It is to set aside the gospel, and place him under another government than that which exists. It sets before him a partial view of the character of God, to which he is required to submit. It keeps back the true motives to submission. It presents not the real and true God, but a different being. It is practising a deception on him, by holding out the idea that God desires his damnation, and he must submit to it ; for God has taken his solemn oath that he desires not the ʻdeath of the wicked, but that he turn from his wickedness and live. It is a slander upon God, and charging God with perjury. Every man under the gospel, knows that God desires sinners to be saved, and it is impossible to hide the fact. The true ground on which salvation should be placed is, that he is not to seek his own salvation, but to seek the glory of God ; not to hold out the idea that God desires or means he should go to hell.

What did the apostles tell sinners, when they inquired what they must do to be saved ? What did Peter tell them at the Pentecost ? What did Paul tell the jailer ? To repent and forsake their selfishness, and believe the gospel. This is what men must do to be saved.

There is another difficulty in attempting to convert men in this way. It is attempting to convert them by the law, and setting aside the gospel. It is attempting to make them holy, without the appropriate influences to make them holy. Paul tried this way, thoroughly, and found it never would answer. In the 7th of Romans, he gives us the result in his own case. It drove him to confess that the law was holy and good, and he ought to obey it ; and there it left him in distress, and crying, "The good that I would, I do not, but the evil that I would not, that I do." The law was not able to convert him, and he cries out, "O wretched man that I am ! who shall deliver me from the body of this death ?" Just here the love of God in sending his Son Jesus Christ, is presented to his mind, and that did the work. In the next chapter he explains it : "What the law could not do in that it was weak through the flesh, God sending his own Son in the likeness of sinful flesh, and for sin, condemned sin in the flesh, that the righteousness of the law might be fulfilled in us, who walk not after the flesh but after the Spirit." The whole Bible testifies that it is only the influence of the gos pel which can bring sinners to obey the law. The law wil never do it. Shutting out from the soul that class of motives which cluster around it from the gospel, will never convert a sinner.

I know there may be some persons who suppose they were converted in this way, and that they have submitted to the law, absolutely, and without any influence from the gospel. But was it ever concealed from them for a moment, that Christ had died for sinners, and that if they should repent and believe, they should be saved ? These motives must have had their influence, for all the time that they think they were looking at the naked law they expected that if they believed they should be saved.

I suppose the error of attempting to convert men by the law, without the gospel, lies here ; in the old Hopkin-sian notion that men, in order to be saved must be willing to be damned. It sets aside the fact, that this world is, and since the fall always has been, under a dispensation of mercy. If we were under a government of mere law, true submission to God would require this. But men are not, in this sense, under the law, and never have been ; for im-mediately after the fall, God revealed to Adam the intima-tions of mercy.

An objection arises here in the mind of some, which I will remove.

Objection. "Is not the offer of mercy, in the gospel, calculated to produce a selfish religion ? "

Answer. The offer of mercy may be perverted, as every other good thing may be, and then it may give rise to a selfish religion. And God knew it would be so, when he revealed the gospel. But observe : Nothing is calculated to subdue the rebellious heart of man, but this very exhibition of the benevolence of God, in the offer of mercy.

There was a father who had a stubborn and rebellious son, and he tried long to subdue him by chastisement. He loved his son, and longed to have him virtuous and obedient. But the child seemed to harden his heart against his repeated efforts. At length the poor father was quite discouraged, and burst out into a flood of convulsive weeping—" My son ! my son ! what shall I do ? Can I save you ? I have done all that I could to save you ; O what can I do more ? " The son had looked at the rod with a brow of brass, but when he saw the tears rolling down his father's furrowed cheeks, and heard the convulsive sobs of anguish from his aged bosom, he too burst into tears, and cried out, " Whip me father ! do whip me, as much as you please, but don't cry !" Now the father had found out the way to subdue that stubborn heart. Instead of holding over him nothing but the iron hand of law, he let out his soul before him ; and what was the effect ? To crush him into hypocritical submission ? No, the rod did that. The gushing tears of his father's love broke him down at once to true submission to his father's will.

So it is with sinners. The sinner braves the wrath of Almighty God, and hardens himself to receive the heaviest bolt of Jehovah's thunder ; but when he sees the *love* of his Heavenly Father's heart, if there is anything that will make him abhor and execrate himself, that will do it, when he sees God manifested in the flesh, stooping to take human nature, hanging on the cross, and pouring out his soul in tears, and bloody sweat, and death. Is this calculated to make hypocrites ? No, the sinner's heart melts, and he cries out, " O, do any thing else, and I can bear it ; but the love of the blessed Jesus overwhelms me." This is the very nature of the mind, to be thus influenced. Instead, therefore, of being afraid of exhibiting the love of God to sinners, it is the only way to make them truly submissive and truly benevolent. The law may make hypocrites ; but nothing but the gospel can draw out the soul in true love to God.

4

LOVE

"Love worketh no ill to his neighbor; therefore love is the fulfilling of the law." Romans 13:10.

IN speaking from these words, I design,

    I. To make some remarks on the nature of love.

    II. To show that love is the whole of religion.

    III. Some things that are not essential to perfect love.

    IV. Some things that are essential.

    V. Some of the effects of perfect love.

I. I am to make some remarks on the nature of love.

1. The first remark I have to make is, that there are various forms under which love may exist.

The two principal forms, so far as religion is concerned, are benevolence and complacency. Benevolence is an affection of the mind, or an act of the will. It is willing good, or a desire to promote the happiness of its object. Complacency is esteem, or approbation of the character of its object. Benevolence should be exercised towards all beings, irrespective of their moral character. Complacency is due only to the good and holy.

2. Love may exist either as an affection or as an emotion.

When love is an affection, it is voluntary, or consists in the act of the will. When it is an emotion, it is involuntary. What we call feelings, or emotions, are involuntary. They are not directly dependent on the will, or controlled by a direct act of will. The virtue of love is mostly when it is in the form of an affection. The happiness of love is mostly when it is in the form of an emotion. If the affection of love be very strong, it produces a high

degree of happiness, but the emotion of holy love is happiness itself.

I said that the emotion of love is involuntary. I do
not mean that the will has nothing to do with it, but that
it is not the result of a mere or direct act of the will. No
man can exercise the emotion of love by merely willing it.
And the emotion may often exist in spite of the will. Individuals often feel emotions rising in their minds, which
they know to be improper, and try by direct effort of will
to banish them from their minds ; and finding that impossible, therefore conclude that they have no control of these
emotions. But they may always be controlled by the will
in an indirect way. The mind can bring up any class of
emotions it chooses, by directing the attention sufficiently
to the proper object. They will be certain to rise in proportion as the attention is fixed, provided the will is right
in regard to the object of attention. So of those emotions
which are improper or disagreeable ; the mind may be rid
of them, by turning the attention entirely away from the
object, and not suffering the thoughts to dwell on it.

3. Ordinarily, the emotions of love towards God are
experienced when we exercise love towards him in the form
of affection.

But this is not always the case. We may exercise good
will towards any object, and yet at times feel no sensible
emotions of love. It is not certain that even the Lord
Jesus Christ exercised love towards God, in the form of
emotion, at all times. So far as our acquaintance with
the nature of the mind goes, we know that a person may
exercise affection, and be guided and be governed by it,
constantly, in all his actions, without any felt emotion of
love towards its object at the time. Thus a husband and
father may be engaged in laboring for the benefit of his
family, and his very life controlled by affection for them,
while his thoughts are not so engaged upon them as to

make him feel any sensible emotions of love to them at the time. The things about which he is engaged may take up his mind so much, that he has scarcely a thought of them, and so he may have no felt emotion towards them, and yet he is all the time guided and governed by affection for them. Observe here, that I use the term, affection, in the sense of President Edwards, as explained by him in his celebrated Treatise on the Will. An affection in his treatise is an act of the will or a volition.

4. Love to our neighbor naturally implies the existence of love to God, and love to God naturally implies love to our neighbor.

The same is declared in the 8th verse, " Owe no man any thing, but to love one another : for he that loveth another hath fulfilled the law. For this, Thou shalt not commit adultery, Thou shalt not kill, Thou shalt not steal, Thou shalt not bear false witness, Thou shalt not covet ; and if there be any other commandment, it is briefly comprehended in this saying, namely, Thou shalt love thy neighbor as thyself." Here it is taken for granted that love to our neighbor implies the existence of love to God, otherwise it could not be said that " he that loveth another hath fulfilled the law." The apostle James recognizes the same principle, when he says, " If ye fulfil the royal law according to the scripture, Thou shalt love thy neighbor as thyself, ye do well." Here love to our neighbor is spoken of as constituting obedience to the whole law. Benevolence, that is, good will to our neighbor, naturally implies love to God. It is love to the happiness of being. So the love of complacency towards holy beings naturally implies love to God, as a being of infinite holiness.

II. I am to show that love is the whole of religion.

In other words, all that is required of man by God consists in love, in various modifications and results. Love is the sum total of all.

1. The first proof I shall offer is, that the sentiment is taught in the text, and many other passages of scripture.

The scriptures fully teach, that love is the sum total of all the requirements, both of the law and gospel. Our Saviour declares that the great command, Thou shalt love the Lord thy God with all thy heart, soul, mind and strength, and thy neighbor as thyself, is the sum total of all the law and the prophets, or implies and includes all that the whole scriptures, the law and the gospel require.

2. God is love, and to love is to be like God, and to be perfect in love is to be perfect as God is perfect.

All God's moral attributes consist in love, acting under certain circumstances and for certain ends. God's justice in punishing the wicked, his anger at sin, and the like, are only exercises of his love to the general happiness of his kingdom. So it is in man. All that is good in man is some modification of love. Hatred to sin, is only love to virtue acting itself out in opposing whatever is opposed to virtue. So true faith implies and includes love, and faith which has no love in it, or that does not work by love, is no part of religion. The faith that belongs to religion is an affectionate confidence in God. There is a kind of faith in God, which has no love in it. The devil has that kind of faith. The convicted sinner has it. But there is no religion in it. Faith might rise even to the faith of miracles, and yet if there is no love in it, it amounts to nothing. The apostle Paul, in the 13th chapter of 1 Corinthians, says, "Though I have the gift of prophecy, and understand all mysteries, and all knowledge ; and though I have all faith, so that I could remove mountains, and have not charity, I am nothing."

Just so it is with repentance. The repentance that does not include love is not "repentance towards God." True repentance implies obedience to the law of love, and consequent opposition to sin.

III. I will mention some things that are not essential to perfect love.

1. The highest degree of emotion is not essential to perfect love.

It is manifest that the Lord Jesus Christ very seldom had the highest degree of emotion of love, and yet he always had perfect love. He generally manifested very little emotion, or excitement. Excitement is always proportioned to the strength of the emotions as it consists in them. The Saviour seemed generally remarkably calm. Sometimes his indignation was strong, or his grief for the hardness of men's hearts ; and sometimes we read that he rejoiced in spirit. But he was commonly calm, and manifested no high degree of emotion. And it is plainly not essential to perfect love, that the emotion of love should exist in a high degree.

2. Perfect love does not exclude the idea of increase in love or growth in grace.

I suppose the growth of the mind in knowledge, to all eternity, naturally implies growth in love to all eternity. The Lord Jesus Christ, in his human nature, grew in stature, and in favor with God and man. Doubtless, as a child, he grew in knowledge, and as he grew in knowledge, he grew in love toward God, as well as in favor with God. His love was perfect when he was a child, but it was greater when he became a man. As a human being, he probably always continued to increase in love to God as long as he lived. From the nature of mind, we see that it may be so with all the saints in glory, that their love will increase to all eternity, and yet it is always perfect love.

3. It is not essential to perfect love, that love should always be exercised towards all individuals alike.

We cannot think of all individuals at once. You cannot even think of every individual of your acquaintance at once.   The degree of love towards an individual depends on the fact that the individual is present to the thoughts.

4. It is not essential to perfect love, that there should be the same degree of the spirit of prayer for every individual, or for the same individual at all times.

The spirit of prayer is not always essential to pure and perfect love.   The saints in heaven have pure and perfect love for all beings, yet we know not that they have the spirit of prayer for any.   You may love any individual with a very strong degree of love, and yet not have the spirit of prayer for that individual.   That is, the Spirit of God may not lead you to pray for the salvation of that individual.   You do not pray for the wicked in hell.   The spirit of prayer depends on the influences of the Holy Ghost, leading the mind to pray for things agreeable to the will of God.   You cannot pray in the Spirit, with the same degree of fervor and faith, for all mankind.   Jesus Christ said expressly, he did not pray for all mankind : " I pray not for the world."   Here has been a great mistake in regard to the spirit of prayer.   Some suppose that Christians have not done all their duty when they have not prayed in faith for every individual, as long as there is a sinner on the earth.   Then Jesus Christ never did all his duty, for he never did this.   God has never told us he will save all mankind, and never gave us any reason to believe he will do it.   How then can we pray in faith for the salvation of all ?   What has that faith to rest on ?

5. Perfect love is not inconsistent with those feelings of languor or constitutional debility, which are the necessary consequence of exhaustion or ill health.

We are so constituted, that excitement naturally and necessarily exhausts our powers.   But love may be perfect, notwithstanding. Though one may feel more disposed to lie down and sleep than to pray, yet his love may be perfect. The Lord Jesus Christ often felt this weariness and ex haustion, when the spirit was still willing, but the flesh **was** weak.

IV. What is essential to perfect love.

1. It implies that there is nothing in the mind **incon-sistent** with love.

No hatred, malice, wrath, envy, or any other malignant emotions that are inconsistent with pure and perfect love.

2. That there is nothing in the life inconsistent with love.

All the actions, words, and thoughts, continually under the entire and perfect control of love.

3. That the love to God is supreme.

The love to God is completely supreme, and so entirely above all other objects, that nothing else is loved in comparison with God.

4. That love to God is disinterested.

God is loved for what he is ; not for his relation to us, but for the excellence of his character.

5. That love to our neighbor should be equal, i.e. that his interest and happiness should be regarded by us of equal value with our own, and he and his interests are to be treated accordingly by us.

V. I am to mention some of the effects of perfect love.

1. One effect of perfect love to God and man will certainly be, delight in self-denial for the sake of promoting the interests of God's kingdom and the salvation of sinners.

See affectionate parents, how they delight in self-denial for the sake of promoting the happiness of their children. There is a father ; he gives himself up to exhausting labor, day by day, and from year to year, through the whole of a long life, rising early, and eating the bread of carefulness continually, to promote the welfare of his family.   And he counts all this self-denial and toil not a grief or a burden. but a delight, because of the love he bears to his **family.**

See that mother ; she wishes to educate her son at college,
And now, instead of finding it painful it is a joy to her to
sit up late and labor incessantly to help him. That is because she really loves her son. Such parents rejoice more
in conferring gifts on their children, than they would in
enjoying the same things themselves. What parent does
not enjoy a piece of fruit more in giving it to his little
child, than in eating it himself ? The Lord Jesus Christ
enjoyed more solid satisfaction in working out salvation for
mankind than any of his saints can ever enjoy in receiving
favors at his hands. He testified that it is more blessed to
give than to receive. This was the joy set before him, for
which he endured the cross and despised the shame. His
love was so great for mankind, that it constrained him to
undertake this work, and sustained him triumphantly
through it.—The apostle Paul did not count it a grief and
a hardship to be hunted from place to place, imprisoned,
scourged, stoned, and counted the offscouring of all things,
for the sake of spreading the gospel and saving souls. It
was his joy. The love of Christ so constrained him, he
had such a desire to do good, that it was his highest delight to lay himself on that altar as a sacrifice to the cause.
Other individuals have had the same mind with the apostle.
They have been known who would be willing to live a
thousand years, or to the end of time, if they could be em-
ployed in doing good, in promoting the kingdom of God,
and saving the souls of men, and willing to forego even
sleep and food to benefit objects they so greatly love.

2. It delivers the soul from the power of legal motives.

Perfect love leads a person to obey God, not because he
fears the wrath of God, or hopes to be rewarded for doing
this or that, but because he loves God and loves to do the
will of God. There are two extremes on this subject. One
class make virtue to consist in doing right, simply because
it is right, without any reference to the will of God, or any

influence from God.   Another class makes virtue to consist in acting from love to the employment, but without
reference to God's authority, as a Ruler and Law-giver.
Both of these are in error.   To do a thing simply because
he thinks it right, and not out of love to God is not virtue.
Neither is it virtue to do a thing because he loves to do it,
with no regard to God's will.   A woman might do certain
things because she knew it would please her husband, but
if she did the same thing merely because she loved to do
it, and with no regard to her husband, it would be no virtue as it repects her husband.   If a person loves God, as
soon as he knows what is God's will, he will do it because
it is God's will.   Perfect love will lead to universal obedience, to do God's will in all things, because it is the will
of God.

3. The individual who exercises perfect love will be
dead to the world.

I mean by this that he will be cut loose from the influence of worldly considerations.   Perfect love will so anni-
hilate selfishness, that he will have no will but the   will
of God, and no interest but God's glory.   He will not be
influenced by public sentiment, or what this and that man
will say or think.   See that woman ! what is she not willing to do from natural affection to her husband ?   She is
willing to cut loose from all her friends, as much as if she
was dead to them, and not pay the least regard to what
they say, and leave all the riches, and honors, and delights
they can offer, to join the individnal whom she loves, and
live with him in poverty, in disgrace, and in exile.   Her
affection is so great that she does it joyfully, and is ready
to go from a palace to any cottage or cave in earth, and be
perfectly happy.   And all that her friends can say against
the man of her affection has not the least influence on her
mind, only to make her cling the more closely to him.
This one *all-absorbing* affection has actually killed all the

influences that used to act on her.   To attempt to influence her by such things is in vain.   There is only one avenue of approach to her mind—only one class of motives move her, and that is through the object of her affection.

So far as the philosophy of mind is concerned, the perfect love of God operates in the same way.   The mind that is filled with perfect love, it is impossible to divert from God, while love continues in exercise.   Take away his worldly possessions, his friends, his good name, his children, send him to prison, beat him with stripes, bind him .ɔ the stake, fill his flesh full of pine knots and set them on fire ; and then leave him his God and he is happy.   His strong affection can make him insensible to all things else. He is as if he were dead to all the world but his God. Cases have been known of marytrs who, while their bodies were frying at the stake, were so perfectly happy in God, as to lose their sense of pain.   Put such a one in hell, in the lake of fire and brimestone, and as long as he enjoys God, and the love of God fills his soul, he is happy.

Who has not witnessed or heard of cases of affection, approaching in degree to what I have described, where a person is in fact dead to all other things, and lives only for the loved object.   How often do you see fond parents, who live for an only child, and when that child dies, wish themselves dead.   Sometimes a husband and wife have such an absorbing affection for each other, that they live for nothing else ; and if the husband dies, the wife pines away and dies also.   The soul-absorbing object for which she lived is gone, and why should she live any longer ?   So, when an individual is filled with the perfect love of God, he wishes to live only to love and serve God ; he is dead to the world, dead to his own reputation, and has no desire to live for any other reason, here, or in heaven, or any where else in the universe, but to glorify God.   He is willing to live, here or any where else, and suffer and labor a thousand years, or to all eternity, if it will glorify God.

I recollect hearing a friend say, often, " I don't know that I have one thought of living a single moment for any other purpose than to glorify God, any more than I should think of leaping right into hell." This was said soberly and deliberately, and the whole life of that individual corresponded with the declaration. He was intelligent, sober-minded, and honest, and I have no doubt expressed what had been the fullest conviction of his mind for years. What was this but perfect love ? What more does any angel in heaven do than this ? His love may be greater in degree, because his strength is greater. But the highest angel could not love more perfectly, than to be able to say in sincerity, " I should as soon think of leaping into hell as of living one moment for any other object but to glorify God." What could Jesus Christ himself say more than that ?

4. It is hardly necessary to say that perfect joy and peace are the natural results of perfect love.

But I wish to turn your attention here to what the apostle says in the 13th chapter of 1 Corinthians, speaking of charity, or love. You will observe that the word here translated " charity " is the same that is in other places rendered *love*. It means love. " Though I speak with the tongues of men and of angels, and have not charity, I am become as sounding brass, or a tinkling cymbal. And though I have the gift of prophecy, and understand all mysteries, and all knowledge ; and though I have all faith so that I could remove mountains, and have not charity, I am nothing." He might have even the faith of miracles, so strong that he could move mountains from their everlasting foundations, and yet have no love. " And though I bestow all my goods to feed the poor, and though I give my body to be burned, and have not charity, it profiteth me nothing." You see how far he supposes a man may go without love. "Charity suffereth long." Long-suffering is meekness under opposition or injury. This is one of the effects of love, to bear great provocations, and not retaliate or revile again. Love is kind, or affectionate in all intercourse with others, never harsh or rude, or needlessly giving pain to any. Love envieth not, never dislikes others because they are more thought of or noticed, more honored or useful, or make greater attainments in knowledge, happiness or piety. Is not puffed up with pride, but always humble and modest. Doth not behave itself unseemly, but naturally begets a pleasant and courteous deportment towards all. However unacquainted the individual may be with the ways of society, who is actuated by perfect love, he always appears well, it is natural to him to be so kind and gentle and courteous. Seeketh not her own, or has no selfishness. Is not easily provoked. This is always the effect of love. See that mother, how long she bears with her children, because she loves them. If you see an individual that is testy, or crusty, easily flying into a passion when anything goes wrong—he is by no means perfect in love, if he has any love. To be easily provoked is always a sign of pride. If a person is full of love, it is impossible to make him exercise sinful anger while love continues. He exercises such indignation as God exercises, and as holy angels feel, at what is base and wrong, but he will not be provoked by it. Thinketh no evil. Show me a man that is always suspicious of the motives of others, and for ever putting the worst construction on the words and actions of his fellow-men, and I will show you one who has the devil in him, not the Holy Ghost. He has that in his own mind which makes him think evil of others. If an individual is honest and simple-hearted himself, he will be the last, to think evil of others. He will not be always smelling

heresy or mischief in others. On the contrary, such persons are often liable to be imposed on by designing men,
not from any want of good sense, but from the effect of
love. They do not suspect evil, where the exterior appears
fair, nor without the strongest proof. Love rejoiceth
not in iniquity, but rejoiceth in the truth. See a man
who exults at his neighbor's fall, or cries out, I told you
so ; and I tell you, that man is far enough from being
perfect in love. Beareth all things, all provocations and
injuries, without revenge, Believeth all things, instead
of being hard to be convinced of what is in favor of others,
is always ready to believe good wherever there is the least
evidence of it. Hopeth all things ; even where there
is reason to suspect evil, as long as there is room for hope,
by putting the best construction upon the thing which it
will bear. Where you see an individual that has not this
spirit, rest assured, he is by no means sincerely in love.
Nay, he has no love at all.

I might pursue this course of thought farther, but have
not time. Love worketh no ill to his neighbor. Mark
that, *no ill!* Perfect love never overreaches, nor defrauds,
nor oppresses, nor does any ill to a neighbor. Would a
man under the influence of perfect love, sell his neighbor
rum ? Never. Would a man that loved God with all his
heart, perfectly, hold his neighbor as a slave ? Love
worketh no ill to his neighbor ; slavery denies him the
wages that he has earned, and perhaps sells him, and tears,
him away from his family, deprives him of the Bible, and
endeavors as far as possible to make him a brute. There
cannot be greater falsehood and hypocrisy, than for a man
who will do that, to pretend that he loves God, now that
light is shed upon this subject, and the attention of men
turned upon it. Will a man hate his own flesh ? How
can he love God that hates or injures his neighbor ?

I designed to remark on one other effect of perfect

love. It uniformly shows itself in great efforts for the sanctification of the church and the salvation of souls. Where a person is negligent or deficient in either of these, he is by no means perfect in love, whatever may be his pretensions.

CONCLUSION

I. You see why it is true, what the apostle James says, "If any man among you seem to be religious, and bridleth not his tongue, but deceiveth his own heart, this man's religion is vain."

The man that professes to be religious, and yet allows himself to speak against his neighbor with an unbridled tongue, to injure his neighbor, deceives himself, if he thinks he loves his neighbor as himself. Strange love!

II. There may be much light in the mind concerning religion, without love.

You often see individuals, who understand a great deal, intellectually, about religion, and can spread it out before others, while it is plain they are not actuated by the spirit of love. They have not the law of kindness on their lips.

III. Those individuals who have much religious knowledge and zeal, without love, are most unlovely and dangerous persons.

They are always censorious, proud, heady, high-minded. They may make a strong impression, but do not produce true religion. They zealously affect you, but not well.

IV. The drift of a man's zeal will determine the character of his religion.

It will show whether the light in his mind is accompanied with love. If it is, his zeal will not be sectarian in its character. Show me a man full of jealousy towards all that do not belong to his sect or party, and there is a man far enough from perfect love.

True love is never denunciatory or harsh. If it has occasion to speak of the faults of others, it does it in kindness, and with sorrow. Perfect love cannot speak in a rough or abusive manner, either to or of others. It will not lay great stress on the mere circumstantials of religion, nor be sticklish for particular measures or forms. Many will contend fiercely either for or against certain things, as for or against new measures ; but if they were full of love they would not do it. The zeal that is governed by perfect love will not spend itself in contending for or against any forms in religion, nor attack minor errors and evils. Love leads to laying stress on the fundamentals in religion. It cleaves to warm-hearted Christians, no matter of what denomination they may be, and loves them, and delights to associate with them.

This zeal is never disputatious, or full of controversy. Find a man who loves to attend ecclesiastical meetings, and enters into all the janglings of the day, and that man is not full of love. To a mind filled with holy love, it is exceedingly painful to go to such meetings, and see ministers dividing into parties, and manœuvring, and caucussing, and pettifogging, and striving for the mastery. Find an individual who loves controversy in the newspapers, he is not full of love. If he was, he would rather be abused, and reviled, and slandered, either in person or by the papers, than turn aside to defend himself or to reply. He would never return railing for railing, but contrariwise blessing. And as much as possible, he would live peaceably with all men.

V. How much that is called religion has no love.

How much of what passes for works of religion, is constrained by outward causes and influences, and not by the inward power of love. It ought to be better understood than it is, that unless love is the mainspring, no matter what the outward action may be, whether praying, praising, giving, or anything else, there is no religion in it.

How much excitement that passes for religion, has no .ove.
How much zeal has no religion in it.   See that man always
full of bitter zeal, and if reproved for it, flying to the example of Paul, when he said, " Thou child of the devil."
If he was under the influence of perfect love, he would see
that his circumstances are so different as not to justify the
exercise of such a spirit.

VI. Those religious excitements which do not consist
in the spirit of love, are not revivals of religion.

Perhaps the church may be much excited, and bustle
about with a great show of zeal, and boisterous noise, but
no tenderness of spirit.   Perhaps, those who go about may
show a spirit of insolence, and rudeness, and pick a quar-
rel with every family they visit.   I once knew a young
man who acknowledged that he aimed at making people
angry, and the reason he assigned was, that it often
brought them under conviction, and so issued in conversion.   And so it might if he should go in and utter horrid blasphemies in their presence, until they were frigh-
tened into a consideration of their own character.   But who
would defend such a conduct on the ground that such was
now and then the result ?   And if this be the character of
the excitement, it may be a revival of wrath, and malice,
and all uncharitableness, but it is not a revival of religion.
I do not mean that when some or many are filled with
wrath, it is certain proof that there is no revival of religion ; but that when the excitement has this prevailing
character, it is not a true revival of religion.   Some among
them may have the spirit of love, but certainly those who
are filled with a bitter disputatious zeal are not truly religious.   Religion may be in some persons revived, but in the
main, in such cases, it is a revival of irreligion.

VII. When persons profess to be converted, if love is
not the ruling feature in their character they are not truly
converted.

However well they may appear in other respects, no matter how clear their views, or how deep their feelings, if they have not the spirit of love to God, and love to man, they are deceived. Let no such converts be trusted.

VIII. See what the world will be, when mankind are universally actuated by a spirit of love.

We learn that the time will come, when there shall be nothing to hurt or destroy, and when the spirit of love will universally prevail. What a change in society! What a change in all the methods of doing business, and in all the intercourse of mankind, when each shall love his neighbor as himself, and seek the good of others as his own? Could one of the saints of the present day revisit the earth at that period, he would not know the world in which he had lived, all things would be so altered. Is it possible, he would exclaim, "that this is the earth; the same earth that used to be so full of jangling, and oppression, and fraud?"

IX. The thing on which the Lord Jesus Christ is bent, is to bring all mankind under the influence of love.

Is it not a worthy object? He came to destroy the works of the devil; and this is the way to do it. Suppose the world was full of such men as Jesus Christ was in his human nature—compare it with what it is now. Would not such a change be worthy of the Son of God? What a glorious end, to fill the earth with love.

X. It is easy to see what makes heaven.

It is love—perfect love. And it is easy to see what makes heaven begun on earth, in those who are full of love. How sweet their temper; what delightful companions; how blessed to live near them: so full of candor, so kind, so gentle, so careful to avoid offence, so divinely amiable in all things!

And is this to be attained by men? Can we love God, in this world with all the heart, and soul, and strength, and mind ? Is it our privilege and our duty to possess the Spirit of Christ—and shall we exhibit the spirit of the devil ? Beloved, let our hearts be set on perfect love, and let us give God no rest till we feel our hearts full of love, and till all our thoughts and all our lives are full of love to God and love to man. O, when will the church come up to this ground ? Only let the church be full of love, and she will be fair as the moon, clear as the sun, and terrible to all wickedness, in high places and low places, as an army with banners.

5

PUBLIC OPINION

"For they loved the praise of men more than the praise of God."
John 12:43.

THESE words were spoken of certain individuals who refused to confess that Jesus was the Christ, because he was extremely unpopular with the scribes and pharisees, and principal people of Jerusalem.

There is a plain distinction between self-love, or the simple desire of happiness, and *selfishness*. Self-love, the desire of happiness and dread of misery, is constitutional ; it is a part of our frame as God made us, and as he intended us to be ; and its indulgence within the limits of the law of God, is not sinful. Whenever it is indulged contrary to the law of God, it becomes sinful. When the desire of happiness or the dread of misery becomes the controlling principle, and we prefer our own gratification to some other greater interest, it becomes selfishness. When, to avoid pain or procure happiness, we sacrifice other greater interests, we violate the great law of disinterested benevolence, it is no longer self-love, acting within lawful bounds, but selfishness.

In my last Friday evening lecture, I described a class of professors of religion, who are moved to perform religious exercises by hope and fear. They are moved sometimes by self-love, and sometimes by selfishness. Their supreme object is not to glorify God, but to secure their own salvation. You will recollect that this class, and the class I had described before as the real friends of God and man, agree in many things, and if you look only at the things in which they agree, you cannot distinguish between them. It is only by a close observation of those things in which they differ, that you can see that the main design of the latter class is not to glorify God, but to secure their own salvation. In that way we can see their supreme object developed, and see that when they do the same things, outwardly, which those do whose supreme object is to glorify God, they do them from entirely different motives, and consequently the acts themselves are, in the sight of God, of an entirely different character.

To-night, I design to point out the characteristics of the third class of professing Christians, who "love the praise of men more than the praise of God."

I would not be understood to imply that a mere regard for reputation has led this class to profess religion. Religion has always been too unpopular with the great mass of mankind to render it a general thing to become professing Christians from a mere regard to reputation. But I mean, that where it is not generally unpopular to become a professor of religion, and will not diminish popularity, but will increase it with many, a complex motive operates—the hope of securing happiness in a future world, and that it may increase reputation here. And thus many are led to profess religion, when after all, on a close examination, it will be seen that the *leading object*, which is prized beyond anything else, is the good opinion of their fellow men. Sooner than forfeit this utterly, they would not profess religion. Their profession turns on this. And although they do profess to be sincere Christians, you may see by their conduct, on close examination, that they will do nothing that will forfeit this good opinion of men. They will not encounter the odium that they must, if they were to give themselves up to root sin out of the world.

Observe, that impenitent sinners are always influenced by one of two things, in all that they do that appears like religion. Either they do them out of regard to mere natural principles as compassion or self-love—principles that

are constitutional in them—or from selfishness.   They are
done either out of regard to their own reputation or happiness, or the gratification of some natural principle in
them, that has no moral character ; and not from the love
of God in them.   They love " the praise of men more than
the praise of God."

I will now mention several things by which you may
detect the true character of the class of persons of whom I
have been speaking ; who make the praise of men their
idol, notwithstanding they profess to love God supremely.
And they are things by which you can detect your own
true characters, if there are any present who properly belong to this class.

1. They do what the apostle Paul says certain persons
did in his day, and for that reason they remained ignorant
of the true doctrine ; they " measure themselves by themselves, and compare themselves among themselves."

There are a vast many individuals, who, instead of
making Jesus Christ their standard of comparison, and the
Bible their rule of life, manifestly aim at no such thing.
They show that they never seriously dreamed of making
the *bible* their standard.   The great question with them
is, whether they do about as many things in religion, and
are about as pious as other people, or as the churches
around them.   Their object is to maintain a *respectable*
profession of religion.   Instead of seriously inquiring for
themselves, what the Bible really requires, and asking
how Jesus Christ would act in such and such cases, they
are looking simply at the common run of professing Christians, and are satisfied with doing what is commendable in
their estimation.   They prove to a demonstration, that
their object is not so much to do what the Bible lays
down as duty, as to do what the great mass of professing
Christians do—to do what is respectable, rather than what
is *right*.

2. This class of persons do not trouble themselves about elevating the standard of piety around them.

They are not troubled at the fact, that the general standard of piety is so low in the church, that it is impossible to bring the great mass of sinners to repentance. They think the standard at the present time is high enough. Whatever be the standard at the time it satisfies them. While the real friends of God and man are complaining of the church, because the standard of piety is so low, and trying to wake up the church to elevate the tone of religion, it all seems to this class of persons like censoriousness, and a meddlesome, uneasy disposition, and as denoting a bad spirit in them. Just as when Jesus Christ denounced the scribes and pharisees, and leading professors of his day, they said, "He hath a devil." "Why, he is denouncing our doctors of divinity, and all our best men, and even dares to call the scribes and pharisees hypocrites, and he tells us that except our righteousness shall exceed theirs, we can in no case enter the kingdom of heaven. What a bad spirit he has."

A large part of the church at the present day have the same spirit, and every effort to open the eyes of the church and to make Christians see that they live so low, so worldly, so much like hyprocrites, that it is impossible the work of the Lord should go on, only excites ill will and occasions reproach. "O," they say, "what a bad spirit he shows, so censorious, and so unkind, surely that is anything but the meek, and kind, and loving spirit of the Son of God." They forget how Jesus Christ poured out his anathemas, enough to make the hills of Judea shake, against those that had the reputation of being the most pious people in that day. Just as if Jesus Christ never said anything severe to anybody, but just fawned over them, and soothed them into his kingdom. Who does not know that it was the hypocritical spirit exhibited by professors of religion,

that roused his soul and moved his indignation, and called
forth his burning torrents of denunciation. He was always
complaining of the very people who were set up as patterns
of piety, and called them hypocrites, and thundered over
their heads the terrible words, "How can ye escape the
damnation of hell!"

It is not wonderful, when so many love the praise of
men more than the praise of God, that there should be excitement when the truth is told. They are very well satisfied with the standard of piety as it is, and think that while
the people are doing so much for Sabbath schools, and
missions, and tracts, that is doing pretty well, and they
wonder what the man would have. Alas! alas! for their
blindness! They do not seem to know that with all this
the lives of the generality of professing Christians are
almost as different from the standard of Jesus Christ as
light is from darkness.

3. They make a distinction between those requirements
of God that are strongly enforced by public sentiment and
those that are not thus guarded.

They are very scrupulous in observing such requirements
as public sentiment distinctly favors, while they easily set
at nought those which public sentiment does not enforce.
You have illustrations of this on every side. I might mention the temperance reformation. How many there are
who yield to public sentiment in this matter what they
never would yield to God or man. At first they waited to
see how it would turn. They resisted giving up ardent
spirits. But when that became popular, and they found
they could do very well with other alcoholic stimulants,
they gave it up. But they are determined to yield no farther than public sentiment drives them. They show that
it is not their object, in joining the temperance society, to
carry out the reform, so as to slay the monster Intemperance; but their object is to maintain a good character.

They love "the praise of men more than the praise of God."

See how many individuals there are, who keep the Sabbath, not because they love God, but because it is respectable. This is manifest, because they keep it while they are among their acquaintances, or where they are known. But when they get where they are not known, or where it will not be a public disgrace, you will find them travelling on the Sabbath.

All those sins that are reprobated by public opinion this class of persons abstain from, but they do other things just as bad which are not thus frowned on. They do those duties which are enforced by public opinion, but not those that are less enforced. They will not stay away from public worship on the Sabbath, because they could not maintain any reputation for religion at all if they did. But they neglect things that are just as peremptorily enjoined in the word of God. Where an individual habitually disobeys any command of God, knowing it to be such, it is just as certain as his soul lives, that the obedience he appears to render, is not from a regard to God's authority, or love to God, but from other motives. He does not, in fact, obey any command of God. The Apostle has settled this question. "Whosoever," says he, "shall keep the whole law, and offend in one point, is guilty of all;" that is, does not truly keep any one precept of the law. Obedience to God's commands implies an obedient state of heart, and therefore nothing is obedience that does not imply a supreme regard to the authority of God. Now, if a man's heart be right, then whatever God enjoins he regards as of more importance than anything else. And if a man regard any thing else of superior weight to God's authority, that is his idol. Whatever we supremely regard—that is our god; whether it be reputation, or comfort, or riches, or honor, or whatever it is that we regard supremely, that

is the god of our hearts.   Whatever a man's reason may
be for habitually neglecting anything which he knows to
be the command of God, or that he sees to be required
to promote the kingdom of Christ, there is demonstration absolute that he regards that as supreme.   There
is nothing acceptable to God in any of his services.   Rest
assured, all his religion is the religion of public sentiment.   If he neglects any thing required by the law of
God, because he can pass along in neglect, and public
sentiment does not enjoin it ; or if he does other things
inconsistent with the law of God, merely because public
opinion does require it, it is a simple matter of fact, that
it is public sentiment to which he yields obedience, in all
his conduct, and not a regard to the glory of God.

How is it with you, beloved ? Do you habitually neglect
any requirement of God, because it is not sustained and
enforced by public sentiment ?   If you are a professor of
religion, it is to be presumed you do not neglect any requirement that is strongly urged by public sentiment.
But, how is it with others ?   Do you not habitually neglect
some duties ?   Do you not live in some practices reputable
among men, that you know to be contrary to the law of
God ?   If you do, it is demonstration absolute that you regard the opinions of men more than the judgment of God.
Write down your name, *hypocrite.*

4. This class of professors are apt to indulge in some
sins when they are away from home, that they would not
commit at home.

Many a man who is temperate at home, when he gets
to a distance, will toss off his glass of brandy and water at
the table, or step up to the bar of a steam-boat and call for
liquor without shame ; or if they are in Europe, they will
go to the theatre.   When I was in the Mediterranean, at
Messina, a gentleman asked me if I would go to the theatre
with him.   " What ! I go to the theatre ?   A minister go to

the theatre ? " " Why," said he, " you are away from home, and no one would know it." " But would not God know it ? " It was plain that he thought, although I was a minister, I could go to the theatre when I was away from home. No matter if God knew it, so long as men did not know it. And how should he get that idea, but by seeing ministers who would do just such things ?

5. Another development of the character of these individuals is, that they indulge themselves in secret sin.

I am now speaking of something, by which you may know yourselves. If you allow yourselves in any sins secretly, when you can get along without having any human being know it, know that God sees it, and that he has already written down your name, *hypocrite.* You are more afraid of disgrace in the eye of mortals, than of disgrace in the eye of God. If you loved God supremely, it would be a small thing to you that any and every body else knew your sins, in comparison with having them known to God. If tempted to any such thing, you would exclaim, " What ! shall I commit sin under the eye of God ? "

6. They indulge in secret omissions of duty, which they would not dare to have known to others.

They may not practise any secret sins, or indulge in those secret pollutions that are spoken of, but they neglect those duties, that if they were known to neglect, it would be called disreputable to their Christian character. Such as secret prayer for instance. They will go to the communion—yes, to the communion !—and appear to be very pious on the Sabbath, and yet, as to private piety, they know nothing of it. Their closet for prayer is unknown to God or man. It is easy to see that reputation is their idol. They dread to lose their reputation more than to offend God.

How is it with you ? Is it a fact, that you habitually omit those secret duties, and are more careful to perform your public duties than private ones ?   Then what is your character ?   Do you need to be told ?   "They loved the praise of men more than the praise of God."

7. The conscience of this class of persons seems to be formed on other principles than those of the gospel.

They seem to have a conscience in those things that are popular, and no conscience at all on those things that are not required by public sentiment.   You may preach to them ever so plainly, their duty, and prove it ever so clearly, and even make them confess that it is their duty, and yet so long as public sentiment does not require it, and it is not a matter of reputation, they will continue on in the same way as before.   Show them a " Thus saith the Lord," and make them see that their course is palpably inconsistent with Christian perfection, and contrary to the interests of the kingdom of Christ, and yet they will not alter.   They make it manifest that it is not the require-ment of God they regard, but the requirement of public opinion.   They love the praise of men more than the praise of God.

8. This class of persons generally dread, very much, the thought of being considered fanatical.

They are ignorant, practically, of a first principle in religion, *that all the world is wrong* !   That the public sentiment of the world is all against God, and that every one who intends to serve God must in the first instance set his face against the public sentiment of the world.   They are to take it for granted, that in a world of rebels, public sentiment is as certainly wrong as that there is a controversy with God.   They have never had their eyes open to this fundamental truth, that the world is wrong, and that God's ways are directly over against their ways.   Consequently, it is true, and always has been true, that " all that will live godly in Christ Jesus shall suffer persecution."   They shall be called fanatical, superstitious, ultras, and the like. They always have been, and they always will be, as long as the world is wrong.

But this class of persons will never go further than is consistent with the opinions of worldly men. They say they must do this and that in order to have influence over such men. Right over against this is the course of the true friends of God and man. Their leading aim is to reverse the order of the world, and turn the world upside down, to bring all men to obey God, and all the opinions of men to conform to the word of God, and all the usages and institutions of the world to accord with the spirit of the gospel.

9. They are very intent on making friends on both sides.

They take the middle course always. They avoid the reputation of being righteous over-much, on the one hand, and on the other hand, of being lax or irreligious. It has been so for centuries, that a person could maintain a reputable profession of religion, without ever being called fanatical. And the standard is still so without ever being called fanatical. And the standard is still so low, that probably the great mass of the protestant churches are trying to occupy this middle ground. They mean to have friends on both sides. They are not set down as reprobates on the one hand, nor as fanatics or bigots on the other. They are "fashionable Christians!" They may be called fashionable Christians for two reasons. One is, that their style of religion is popular and fashionable; and the other is, that they generally follow worldly fashions. Their aim in religion is not to do anything that will disgust the world. No matter what God requires, they are determined to be so prudent as not to bring on them the censures of the world, nor offend the enemies of God. They have manifestly more regard to men than to God. And if they are ever so circumstanced that they must do that which will displease their friends and neighbors, or

offend God, they will offend God. If public sentiment
clashes with the commands of God, they will yield to public sentiment.

10. They will do more to gain the applause of men
than to gain the applause of God.

This is evident from the fact, that they will yield obedience only to those requirements of God which are sustained by public opinion. Although they will not exercise
self-denial to gain the applause of God, yet they will exercise great self-denial to gain the applause of men. The
men that gave up ardent spirits, because public sentiment
rendered it necessary, will give up wine also, whenever a
public sentiment sufficiently powerful shall demand it;
and not till then.

11. They are more anxious to know what are the opinions of men about them, than to know what is God's
opinion of them.

If one of this class is a minister, and preaches a sermon, he is more anxious to know what the people thought
of it, than to know what God thought of it. And if he
make anything like a failure, the disgrace of it with men
cuts him ten times more than the thought that he has dishonored God, or hindered the salvation of souls. Just so
with an elder, or a member of the church, of this class.
If he pray in a meeting, or exhort, he is more concerned
to know what is thought of it, than to know how God is
pleased.

If such a one has some secret sin found out, he is vastly
more distressed about it because he is disgraced than because God is dishonored. Or if he fall into open sin, when
he comes to be met with it, he cares as much again about
the disgrace as about the sin of it.

They are more anxious about their appearance in the
eyes of the world, than in the eyes of God. Females of
this character are vastly more anxious, when they go to

church, how the body shall appear in the eyes of men, than
how the heart shall appear in the eyes of God. Such a one
will be all the week engaged in getting everything in order,
so as to make her person appear to advantage, and perhaps
will not spend half an hour in her closet, to prepare her
heart to appear before God in his courts. Every body can
see, at a glance, what this religion is, the moment it is
held up to view. Nobody is at a loss to say what that
man's or that woman's name is—it is *hypocrite*. They
will go into the house of God with their hearts dark
as midnight, while every thing in their external appearance is comely and decent. They must appear well in the
eyes of men, no matter how that part is on which God
fixes his eye. The heart may be dark, and disordered, and
polluted, and they care not, so long as the eye of man de-
tects no blemish.

12. They refuse to confess their sins in the manner
which the law of God requires, lest they should lose their
reputation among men.

If they are ever required to make confession of more
than they think consistent with their reputation, they are
more anxious as to how it will affect their character, than
to know whether God is satisfied.

Search your hearts, you that have made confessions,
and see which most affects your minds, the question what
God thought of it, or what men thought of it. Have you
refused to confess what you knew God required, because
it would hurt your reputation among men? Will not God
judge your hearts? Only be honest now, and let it be answered.

13. They will yield to custom what they know to be
injurious to the cause of religion, and to the welfare of
mankind.

A striking instance of this is found in the manner of
keeping new year's day. Who does not know that the cus-

tomary manner of keeping new year's day, setting out their
wine and their rich cake and costly entertainments, and
spending the day as they do, is a waste of money, hurtful
to health, and injurious to their own souls and to the interests of religion ? And yet they do it. Shall we be told
that persons who will do this when they *know* it is injurious, supremely love God ? I care not who attempts to
defend such a custom, it is wrong, and every Christian
must know it to be so. And those who persist in it when
they know better, demonstrate that a supreme regard to
God is not their rule of life.

14. They will do things of doubtful character, or things
the lawfulness of which they strongly doubt, in obedience
to public sentiment.

You will recollect that on the evening of the first day
of the year I took up this subject, and showed that those
who do things of doubtful character, of the lawfulness of
which they are not satisfied, are condemned for it in the
sight of God.

15. They are often "ashamed" to do their duty, and
so much ashamed that they will not do it.

Now when a person is so much ashamed to do what
God requires as not to do it, it is plain that his own reputation is his idol. How many do you find who are ashamed
to acknowledge Jesus Christ, ashamed to reprove sin in
high places or low places, and ashamed to speak out when
religion is assailed ! If they supremely regarded God,
could they ever be ashamed of doing their duty ? Suppose a man's wife were calumniated, would he be ashamed
to defend his wife ? By no means. If his children were
abused, would he be ashamed to take their part ? Not if
he loved them ; it would not be shame that would deter
him from defending his wife or children. If a man was
friendly to the administration of the government of his
country, and heard it calumniated, would he be ashamed

to defend it ? He might not think it expedient to speak, for other reasons ; but if he was a true friend to the government, he would not be " ashamed " to speak in its behalf, anywhere.

Now such persons as I am speaking of, will not take decided ground when they are among the enemies of truth, where they would be subject to reproach for doing it. They are very bold for the truth when among its friends, and will make a great display of their courage. But when put to the trial, they will sell the Lord Jesus Christ, or deny him before his enemies, and put him to open shame, rather than rebuke wickedness, or speak out in his cause among his enemies.

16. They are opposed to all encroachments on their self-indulgence, by advancing light on practical subjects.

They are much disturbed by every new proposal that draws on their purses, or breaks in upon their habitual self-indulgence. And you may talk as much, and preach as much in favor of it as you please, there is only one way to reach this kind of people, and that is by creating a new public sentiment. When you have brought over, by the power of benevolence and of conscience, a sufficient number in the community to create a public sentiment in its favor, then they will adopt your new proposals, and not before.

17. They are always distressed at what they call the " ultraism " of the day.

They are much afraid the ultraism of the present day will destroy the church. They say we are carrying things too far, and we shall produce a reaction. Take, for instance, the Temperance Reformation. The true friends of temperance now know, that alcohol is the same thing, wherever it is found, and that to save the world and banish intemperance, it is necessary to banish alcohol in all its forms. The pinch of the Temperance Reformation has never yet been decided. The mass of the community have never been called to any self-denial in the cause. The place where it will pinch is, when it comes to the question, whether men will exercise SELF-DENIAL to crush the evil. If they may continue to drink wine and beer, it is no self-denial to give up ardent spirits. It is only changing the form in which alcohol is taken, and they can drink as freely as before. Many friends of the cause, when they saw what multitudes were rushing into it, were ready to shout a triumph. But the real question is not yet tried. And multitudes will never yield, until the friends of God and man can form a public sentiment so strong as to crush the character of every man who will not give it up. You will find many doctors of divinity and pillars of the church, who are able to drink their wine, that will stand their ground, and no command of God, no requirement of benevolence, no desire to save souls, no pity for bleeding humanity, will move such persons, until you can form a public sentiment so powerful as to force them to it, on penalty of loss of reputation. For they love the praise of men.

And it is a query now in my mind, a matter of solemn and anxious doubt, whether in the present low state of piety and decline of revivals of religion in the church, a public sentiment can be formed, so powerful as to do this. If not, we shall be driven back. The Temperance Reformation, like a dam of sand, will be swept away, the floodgates will be opened again, and the world will go reeling—down to hell. And yet thousands of professors of religion, who want to enjoy public respect and at the same time enjoy themselves in their own way, are crying out as if they were in distress at the ultraism of the times !

18. They are often opposed to men, and measures, and things, while they are unpopular and subject to reproach, and when they become popular, fall in with them.

Let an individual go through the churches in any section, and wake them up to a revival of religion, and while he is little known, these persons are not backward to speak against him. But let him go on, and gain influence, and they will fall in and commend him and profess to be his warmest friends. It was just so with Jesus Christ. Before his death, he had a certain degree of popularity. Multitudes would follow him, as he went through the streets, and cry " Hosanna, Hosanna ! " But observe, they never would follow him an atom farther than his popularity followed him. As soon as he was arrested as a criminal, they all turned round and began to cry, " Crucify him, crucify him ! "

This class of persons, as they set with the tide one way, when a man is reproached, so they will set with the tide the other way when he comes to be honored. There is only one exception. And that is, when they have become so far committed to the opposition, that they cannot come round without disgrace. And then they will be silent, until another opportunity comes up for letting out the burning fires that are rankling within them.

Very often a revival in a church, when it first begins, is opposed by certain members of the church. They do not like to have such things carried on, they are afraid there is too much animal excitement, and the like. But the work goes on ; and by-and-by they seem to fall in and go with the multitude. At length the revival is over, and the church grows cold again, and before long you will find this class of persons renewing their opposition to the work, and as the church declines they press their opposition, and perhaps, in the end, induce the church itself to take ground against the very revival which they had so much enjoyed. This is the very way in which individuals have acted in regard to revivals in this country. There are many such cases. They were awed by public sentiment and made to

bow down to the revival, while it was in its power, but by-
and-by, as the revival declines, they begin to let out the
opposition that is in their hearts, and which was suppressed
for a time because the revival was popular.

It has been just so in regard to the cause of missions.
in a degree, and if anything should turn up, unfavorable
to missions, so as to break the present power of public
sentiment in their favor, you would find plenty of these
fair weather supporters turning to the opposition.

19. If any measure is proposed to promote religion they
are very sensitive and scrupulous not to have anything done
that is unpopular.

If they live in a city, they ask what will the other
churches think of such a measure ?   And if it is likely to
bring reproach on their church or their minister, in view
of the ungodly, or in view of the other churches, they are
distressed about it.   No matter how much good it will do,
or how many souls it will save, they do not want to have
anything done to injure the respectability of their church.

20. This class of persons never aim at forming a public sentiment in favor of perfect godliness.

The true friends of God and man are always aiming at
forming public sentiment, and correcting public sentiment,
on all points where it is wrong.   They are set, with all
their hearts, to search out all the evils in the world, and to
reform the world, and drive out iniquity from the earth.
The other class are always following public sentiment as
it is, and feeling after the course of the tide, to go that
way, shrinking back from everything that goes in the face
of public sentiment.   And they are ready to brand as im-
prudent, or rash, any man or anything, that goes to stem
the tide of public sentiment and turn it the other way.

6

SELF DENIAL

"And he said unto them all, If any man will come after me, let him deny himself, and take up his cross daily, and follow me." Luke 9:23.

IN order to understand this solemn declaration of our Lord, the first important point to be ascertained is this, *What is the true idea of taking up the cross and denying one's self?*

This question presupposes the existence of appetites and propensities which call for indulgence, and then it means, obviously, that in some cases this indulgence must be refused. This is the precise point of the text—a man who will follow Christ must deny himself in the sense of denying the gratification of all appetites and propensities whenever and how far soever such gratifications are forbidden by the law of benevolence. All impulses towards self-indulgence, whether in the line of avoiding things we fear or seeking things we love, must be denied, and ruled down by a determined will, whenever indulgence is not demanded, but is forbidden by the law of love. Within the limits of God's law, these constitutional appetites may be indulged; beyond those limits, they must be denied. At whatever point they run counter to the law of love to God or love to man, they must be put down.

The thing demanded, therefore, by this law of Christ's kingdom is, that you consult and obey the will of Christ in this whole matter of self-indulgence; that you obey neither desire nor appetite—that you never gratify your love of approbation—never seek any forms of personal enjoyment *in disobedience to Christ*. You must never do this where duty is known, lest you displease God, for plainly He has rightful control over all your powers.

Under this principle you must do all your duty to your fellow-men—whether to their bodies or to their souls, denying all those worldly desires and propensities which would conflict with this duty, making Jesus Christ Himself your model and his expressed will your perpetual rule.

The question will arise in many minds, Why does Christ demand of us self-denial?

Is it because God loves to see us self-mortified—because He takes pleasure in crucifying the sensibilities to enjoyment which He has given us? By no means. But the true answer is to be found in the fact that He has made us rational and moral beings—our rational faculties being intended for the control of our entire voluntary activities, and our moral nature rendering us properly responsible for the self-control which God requires. In the lower orders of creation around us, we see animals void of moral responsibility because they are constituted irrational and incapable of responsible moral action. To them, propensity must be law, because they can know no other. But we have a higher law to obey than they. Their highest good is promoted by their obedience to mere physical law; but not so with us. Our sensibilities are blind, and therefore were never intended to be our rule of life. To supply such a rule, God has given us intelligence and conscience. Appetite, therefore, cannot be our rule, while it can and must be the rule of all the lower, irrational animals.

Now it is a fact that our sensibilities are out of harmony with our conscience, often clamoring for indulgence which both reason and conscience forbid.

If we give ourselves up to the sway of appetite and unguided sensibility, we are surely misled. These appetites grow worse by indulgence; a fact which of itself shows that God never intended them to be our rule. Often artificial appetites are formed; of such a nature, moreover, as to be exceedingly pernicious in their effects.

Hence we are thrown into a state of warfare. Constant appeals are made to us to arouse our propensities to indulgence; and, over against these, constant appeals are made by the law of God and the voice of our reason, urging us to deny ourselves and find our highest good in obeying God. God and reason require us to withstand the claims of appetite sternly and firmly. Note here that God does not require this withstanding, without vouchsafing his aid in the conflict. It is remarkable how the resolute opposition of any appetite, in the name of Christ and under the demands of conscience, will readily overcome it. Cases often occur in

which the most clamorous and despotic of these artificial appetites are ruled down by the will, under the
demands of conscience and with the help of God.   At
once they lie all subdued, and the mind remains in
sweet peace.

Here let us consider more attentively that we are
conscious of having a spiritual and moral nature as
well as a physical. We have a conscience, and we
have affections correlated to God as truly as we have
affections correlated to earthly things.   There is a
beauty in holiness, and there are things correlated to
our spiritual tastes as truly as to our physical.   Under
proper care and effort, our religious nature may be developed towards God, even as our physical nature is
towards earthly objects.   We are social beings in our
earthly relations, and not less so in our spiritual nature.
We are social spiritually as well as physically, though
we may not be aware of it, because our spiritual soci-
ality may have been utterly uncultivated and undevel-
oped.   But we really need divine communion with God
and social fellowship with our Infinite Maker.   Prior
to regeneration this moral capacity of ours is a waste.
All men have a conscience and may be aware of it,
but they have no spiritual affections towards God, and
hence they assume that religion must be a very dry
thing.   They cannot see how they can enjoy God's
presence and prayer.   They are all awake to earthly
fellowship and friendship, but dead to fellowship and
friendship with God.   Their love in the form of affection has been drawn out towards man, but not towards
God.   They seem not aware that they have a nature

capable of being developed in loving affections towards their divine Father. Hence they do not see how they can ever enjoy religion and religious duties. The coldness of death comes over their souls when they think of it.

This spiritual side of our nature needs to be cultivated. It has been so long kept back and crushed down, it greatly needs to be brought up. But, in order to do this and develop the spiritual side of our nature, it is indispensable that the worldly side be crushed and brought under. For flesh is a dangerous foe to grace. There is no harmony, but only repellency and antagonism, between the earthly affections and the heavenly. Unless we subdue the flesh we shall die. It is only when, through the Spirit, we mortify the deeds of the body that we can live.

The Roman church has in past ages distinguished itself for its mortifications of the flesh—externally considered. These mortifications have thrown off the Protestant world into the opposite extreme. Among all the Protestant sermons I have heard, I do not recollect one on the subject of bearing the cross and denying one's self. I must think that this subject is exceedingly neglected among our Protestant churches. Papal Rome having run wild with this idea, Protestants have taken fright and run off into the opposite extreme. Therefore we need a special effort to guard against this tendency and to bring us back to reason, sense, and Scripture.

Until I was converted I never knew that I had any religious affections. I did not even know that I had any capacity for spontaneous, deep, outgushing emotions towards God. This was indeed a dark and fearful ignorance, and you may readily suppose I knew little of real joy while my soul was so perfectly ignorant of the very idea of real spiritual joy. But, I take it, this absence of all right ideas of God is by no means uncommon. If you search, you will find this to be the common experience of unconverted men.

We all know that the gratification of our animal nature is pleasure—not of the highest sort indeed, yet it is a kind of pleasure. How much more must the gratification of our nobler moral affections be joyful! When the soul comes to feast on its spiritual affections, it begins to taste real happiness—a bliss like that of heaven! I fear many have never comprehended what the Bible means by "*blessedness*."

Now let it be well considered that the spiritual side of our nature can be developed and gratified only by a benevolent crossing of our appetites—a crossing of them, I mean, under the demands of real benevolence towards our fellow-men and towards God. This must be our aim; for if we make our personal happiness the end, we can never attain to the exalted joy of true fellowship with God.

It is curious to see how the sensibility is related to self-denial, so that denying ourselves from right motives becomes the natural and necessary means of developing our spiritual affections. Beginning with taking up the cross, one goes on, from step to step, ruling down self-indulgences and self-gratification, and opening his heart more and more to fellowship with God and to the riper experience of his love.

A further reason why men should deny themselves, is that it is *intrinsically right*. The lower appetites *ought not* to govern us; the higher laws of our nature ought to. The evidence of this is simply the evidence which proves it to be the duty of beings created rational to use their reason, and not degrade themselves down to the level of beasts.

Another reason is that we can well afford it, for we are surely the gainers by it. I admit that when we resist and deny the demands of self-indulgence, it goes a short way, and on a small scale, *against happiness;* but on the spiritual side we gain immensely, and immensely more than we lose. The satisfaction which arises from real self-denial is precious. It is rich in quality and deep and broad as the ocean in amount.

Many think that if they would find pleasure they must seek it directly and make it their direct object, seeking it moreover in the gratification of their appetites. They seem to know no other form of happiness but this. It would seem that they never have conceived the idea that the only way to enjoy themselves really is to deny self, fully up to the demands of right, reason, and of God's revealed will. Yet this is the most essential law of real happiness. Where shunning the cross begins, true religion ends. You may pray in your family, you may sternly rebuke sin wherever it is disagreeable to yourself, and do all this without Christian self-denial; but while living in habits of self-indulgence, you cannot stand up for Christ and do your duty everywhere manfully, and especially you will be all weakness when the path of duty leads you where your feelings will be wounded. And no man can expect to escape such emergencies always. If, then, you would maintain the path of duty without swerving, and enjoy real life and blessedness, you must determine to deny yourself wherever God and reason demand it, and fully up to the extent of those demands. So will you gain more than you can lose. If you are firm and determined, your path will be easy and joyous.

It often happens that the entire drift of a Christian's feelings is towards self-indulgence, so that if he allowed himself to be guided by his feelings he would surely make shipwreck of his soul. God, on his part, shuts him up to simple faith. Then if he follows the Lord's guidance, he will triumph, and all suddenly his "soul is like the chariots of Amminadab." A case in point is now before my mind of a man who once lived here. After a period of Christian life, he went from our place, backslid from God sorely, became almost an infidel, quite a Swedenborgian, became wealthy, and just when you might suppose him to have gained the heights of earthly happiness, and when he supposed so himself, he became, instead, completely wretched. He was forced to fall back upon himself, and say, I must return to God and do his will—the whole of it, whatever it may be, or I shall utterly perish. I will, said he, put an extinguisher upon every worldly affection. Nothing that is hostile to God's will shall be tolerated a moment. No sooner had he done this, than all his religious life and joys came back again. Then his wife and neighbors began to say of him, "He is indeed a new man in Christ Jesus." From that day, the peace of God ruled in his heart, and his cup of joy was full to overflowing. Any man, therefore, can afford to deny himself, since thereby he opens his heart to the joys of immortal life and peace. This is the only way of real happiness.

This subject explains many of the otherwise strange facts of Christian experience. Here is one man who cannot pray before his family. Inquire more deeply into his case, and you will probably find that he cannot enjoy anything in religious duty. Inquire yet further into the cause, and you will find that he does not deny himself, but lives under the laws of self-indulgence. Poor man, he cannot please God so.

Another cannot come out and confess Christ before men. The truth probably is that he has not made up his mind to deny himself at all. On the contrary, he really denies Christ. He shuns the cross. Ah, that is not the way to heaven. In that path you can have no communion with God. Try it a thousand times, and you will still find the same result,—no peace, and no communion with God.

Our text says, "Take up your cross *daily*." So you must. This is the only possible way of holy living. And it must be done firmly, sternly, and continually. It must be made your life-work, save as you gain a respite by substantial victory over your propensities to self-indulgence. Let a man attempt to rule down the appetite for alcoholic drinks, and do it at special seasons only, say once a day, or once in a week, while all the rest of the time he gives himself to full indulgence, he must utterly fail. He never can succeed unless he takes up his cross *daily* and bears it all the time. Absolutely he *must* persevere, or his efforts are all for naught. Precisely in proportion as we sternly take up our cross, it grows light and we grow strong to bear it. When a man indulges himself in tobacco, each day's indulgence makes him more a slave. On the contrary, each successive day's abstinence makes him more a conqueror. If a man resolutely declares, By the help of God, no lust, no appetite, shall have dominion over me, then, holding on, he comes off conqueror. The more firmly you adhere to this principle, and the more steadily you rule down the clamors for self-indulgence, so much the more speedily and surely do you gain the victory. Although at first you take up this work tremblingly, if you hold on, you will gain ground. These appetites will take less and less hold upon you. Bearing your cross will itself make you strong for your toil in the Christian life.

·Shunning the cross grieves the Spirit. If you neglect duty, if you fail to pray in your family, omitting it perhaps because you have company present, you may be very sure the Spirit of God· is grieved. Satan throws these temptations in your path, and you give him every advantage against you. You will perhaps try to pray while in this state; but, oh, God is not with you! You have been placed where you should have done some things unpleasant to flesh and blood; you evaded the claims of present duty; you went to bed at night without doing your duty. How was it then with your soul? Did not dark clouds shut off the light of God's face?

Did you have any comfort of his presence? or any communion with your Saviour? Pause and ask your heart for the answer.

CONCLUSION

1.   So long as the religious sensibilities are not developed, men will of course feel a strong demand for worldly affections. What do they know about the religious affections of the heart? What do they know of real love to God, or of the consciousness of the Spirit's witness to their hearts that they are God's children? Really nothing. They have never crossed their sensual propensities. Of course they have not taken the first step towards developing the heavenly affections of the heart. Consequently all their enjoyments are earthly. Their hearts are only below. But just in proportion as they deny themselves do they fall into adjustment to their spiritual nature.

2.   It is a great and blessed thing for the Christian to find his nature conformed progressively more and more to God; to find it manifestly coming around right, and adjusting itself, under divine grace, to the demands of benevolence.

3.   Crossbearing persisted in, brings out a ripe spiritual culture. The soul longs intensely for spiritual manifestations, and loves communion with God. Hear him say, How sweet the memory of those scenes when my soul lay low before God! How did my heart enjoy his presence! Now I am always sensible of an aching void unless God be there.

4.   When men go about to seek enjoyment as an

end, they surely miss it. All such seeking must certainly be in vain. Benevolence leads the soul out of itself, and sets it upon making others happy. So real blessedness comes.

5. Your usefulness as Christians will be as your crossbearing and as your firmness in this course of life; for your knowledge in spiritual things, your spiritual vitality, your communion with God and, all in one word, your aid from the Holy Ghost, must turn upon the fidelity with which you deny yourself.

6. If you have once known the blessedness of spiritual life, and your heart has been moulded into the image of the heavenly, you can no longer return to the miserable flesh-pots of Egypt. There is no longer any possibility of your enjoying earthly things as the portion of your soul. Let that be considered settled. Abandon at once and forever all further thought of finding your joys in worldly, selfish indulgences.

7. To the young, let me say, your sensibilities are quick, and lean to worldly things. Now is the time for you to be stern in dealing with your self-indulgent spirit before you have gone too far ever to succeed. Are you strongly tempted to give way to self-indulgence? Remember it is an unalterable law of your nature that you must seek your peace and blessedness in God. You cannot find it elsewhere. You must have Jesus for your friend, or be eternally friendless. Your very nature demands that you seek God as your God— the King of your life—the Portion of your soul for happiness. You cannot find Him such to you, save as you

deny yourself, take up your daily cross, and follow Jesus.

8.   To those of you who, being yet in your sins, cannot conceive how you can ever enjoy God, and cannot even imagine how your heart can cleave to God, and call Him a thousand endearing names, and pour out your heart in love to Jesus, let me beg of you to consider that there *is* such communion with God—there *is* such joy of his presence, and you may have it at the the price of self-denial and whole-hearted devotion to Jesus;—not otherwise.   And why should you not make this choice ?   Already you are saying, Every cup of worldly pleasure is blasted—dried up and worthless. Then let them go.   Bid them away, and make the better choice of pleasures that are purer far, and better, and which endure forever.

7

FOLLOWING CHRIST

"Jesus saith unto him. If I will that he tarry till I come, what is that to thee? Follow thou me."   John 21:22.

THESE words Christ spake to Peter.   He had previously given Peter to understand that in his advanced life his liberty would be restrained, and that he would have the honor of glorifying God by a martyr's death.   A question arose in Peter's mind—more curious than wise—how it would fare with his fellow-disciple, John.   So he inquires: "Lord, what shall this man do?"   Gently rebuking this idle inquisitiveness, Jesus replied, "If I will that he tarry till I come, what is that to thee?   Follow thou Me."

This reply involves a principle, and hence it has a wide practical application.   It is really addressed to us.

Assuming it to be thus addressed to all at the present day, what does it teach?   What does Jesus say to *us*?

Suppose He stood where I do this moment, and you knew it to be Jesus Himself, and saw that He was preparing to speak.   You see the halo of glory around his head; you note the blending of meekness and majesty that identifies Him most fully as one like unto the Son of God, and your whole soul is moved within you

117

to catch every word He may utter. Oh, what an earnest expectation! If He were to speak in this house, you would hear the ticking of that clock more plainly than you now do. If you chanced not to catch every word distinctly, you would ask one and another, What did He say? What was that?

He speaks, you observe, in the form of a positive command; what is this command? Remember, if it be the Lord Jesus Christ, He has the *right* to command. Who else in earth or heaven has this right more absolutely than He? It must be of the utmost consequence to us to know what He does command us. Whatever it be, it must vitally affect our well-being both to know and to do it. Words from one so benevolent must be for our good. Certainly, He never did speak but He said things for the good of those to whom He spake.

It must also be for the general good; for the Great King and Lord of all never overlooks what pertains to the general good.

Moreover, it must be safe to obey. Certainly; how can it be otherwise? Did it ever happen that any man obeyed Him and found it unsafe?

Of course it must be our DUTY to obey. How can it be that Christ shall ever command us, and we be not bound solemnly to obey Him?

Also, it must be *possible* for us to obey. Did Christ ever enjoin impracticable things? Could He possibly do a thing so unreasonable?

All these points must be assumed and admitted. How can we ever doubt a moment on any one of them?

This, then, is the state of the case. What, now, should be the attitude of our minds? Manifestly this, Let Him speak; we will surely listen and obey. What does He say? Every word He says, I know, will be infinitely good. Let me catch every intimation of his will. "His words shall be sweeter to my taste than honey or the honey-comb."

But will any of you turn away, saying, "I don't care what He says"? Will you not rather feel this, "Let Him say what He will, it is all good, and I will surely hear and obey it"?

If such be your attitude towards Him, then we are ready to examine what He says. Observe, He gives us *something to be done*, and, moreover, something to be *done by yourself.* No matter just now to you what others may do, or what God's providence may allot to them. "What is that to thee?" It has always been the temptation of the human heart to look at the duties of others rather than one's own. You must resist and put down this temptation. Christ has work for *you* to do, and it becomes you to address yourself earnestly to do it. Observe, also, that it is to be done *now.* He gives you no furlough, not even to go home and bid farewell to those of your house. He can take no excuse for delay.

Now let us ask, What is this thing which He requires? He says, "*Follow thou Me.*" What does this mean? Must I leave my home? Must I abandon my business? Am I to change my residence? Am I to follow Him all over the land?

The latter meaning was plainly the true one when

Jesus dwelt among men in human flesh. He then called certain men to follow Him as his servants and disciples, and they were to attend Him in all his journeyings—to go where He went and to stop where He stopped. They were to aid Him in his missionary work.

Now, Christ is no longer here in human flesh; and therefore following Him cannot have precisely that physical sense. Yet now, no less than then, it implies that you obey his revealed will, and do the things that please Him. Now, you are to imitate his example and follow his instructions. By various methods, He still makes known his will, and you are to follow whithersoever He leads. You must accept Him as the Captain of your salvation, and let his laws control all your life. He comes to save his people from their sins and from the ruin that sin, unforgiven, must bring down; and you must accept Him as such a Saviour. This is involved in following Him.

But let us here inquire somewhat more fully, *What is implied in obeying this command?*

Of course it implies confidence in Him who commands—a confidence in the exercise of which you commit yourself fully to obey Him and trust all consequences to his disposal. There can be no hearty, cheerful obedience without this implicit confidence.

It implies, also, a willingness to be saved by Him— that is, *saved from sin*. You make no reservation of favorite indulgences; you go against all sin and set yourself earnestly to withstand every sort of temptation.

It involves also a present decision to follow Him through evil or good report—whatever the effect may be on your reputation. You are ready to make sacrifices for Christ, rejoicing to be counted worthy to suffer shame for his name.

It is a very common fault to admit what Christ requires, yet to fail very much in doing it. This is saying, I go, sir,—but going not. Such a man does not follow Christ.

He requires *immediate* action. He has work for you to do *to-day*, and He demands of you that you commit yourself to full obedience.

Let us next inquire, WHY *shall we follow Him?*

Suppose Christ were here personally and from this desk announced this command, Follow thou Me. Would you ask to know *why?* You could very soon assign some weighty reasons. Your own mind would suggest them. And do you know any reasons why you should *not* follow Him? I presume it is settled in every mind why you should obey this command, now and here, without one moment's delay. Is there any of you that can assign any reason why you should not obey this command? Does any of you doubt at all whether this be your duty? Can you think of any reason why it is not?

Then it must be your duty, and you ought to do it. The matter should lie in your mind thus, If this is my duty, of course I must do it at once. Doing duty is the business of my life.

You owe it to Jesus Christ to follow Him. If you are a student, none the less should you follow Jesus everywhere. See that young man. You ask him why he goes to college; what does he say? Does he say, Because I would be better prepared to teach men about Jesus Christ? Coming to his teachers, does he say, Give me an education; give me all the discipline of mind and heart you can, that I may be the better able to teach and preach Jesus Christ? Tell me all you know of Christ; pray for me that God may teach my heart the whole gospel; is this what he says? In this sort of way should a Christian student follow Christ.

Do you not owe this to Him? Can any one of you deny this? Have you any right to live to yourselves? If you could gain some good for the moment, could you think it *right* to have your own way, and disown Christ? What if you were to gain the whole world and lose your own soul?

You owe it to yourself to take care of your own soul. God lays on you the responsibility of saving your own soul, and you must bear it. No man can bear that responsibility for you. You must bear it for yourself alone.

You owe it to your friends to follow Christ. You have friends over whom you may exert a precious influence. For their sakes you ought to know Christ, that you may lead them also to follow Him. You have friends also who have done much for you and have loved you much. It is due from you to them that you should follow Christ. You owe it to your father and mother. Are they praying souls? It is due to the sympathy they feel for you and to the strong desire they have for your salvation. If they have never prayed, it is time they did, and time that you should lead them to Christ.

You owe it to the whole world. There are millions who know not Jesus, some of whom you might teach so that they shall not die and never have known Him.

One more thought as to yourself. Such as you make yourself by obeying or not obeying this precept, you will be to all eternity. What you do in this matter will have its fruits on your destiny long after the sun and stars shall have faded away. You have no right to live so that, when you die, men shall say, There goes from earth one nuisance, and hell has more sin in it now than it ever had before.

Again: this is the only path of peace. If you would have peace, you must seek and find it here. Here thousands have found it; but none ever found it anywhere else.

Jesus Christ says to you, "*Follow thou Me.*" Will you set yourself to find some excuse? What are your excuses?

Do you say, "There are so many opinions among men, I do not know what to do"?

Ah! but you *do know*. It is only a pitiful pretence when you say you don't know your duty. Who of you does not know enough to be simple-hearted and to go on in duty and please God? No opinions of men need stumble you if you simply follow Christ. You talk about the various opinions among Christian sects;—but, differ much as they may in lesser matters, on the great things of salvation they are all agreed. They all agree essentially, that to follow Christ in confidence and simple love is the whole of duty, and will ensure his approbation. Follow this simple direction, and all will be well with you.

But some will say, "I believe all will be saved."

You do, indeed! Will they all become like Christ before they die? Do they all in fact become holy in this world? Christ is in heaven. Can you go there unless you become first like Him in heart and in life?

What is such a belief good for? Often has this question been forced on my mind in Boston, What is this belief that all men will be saved, good for? People plead this belief as their excuse for not following Christ. They say, "No need to trouble ourselves with following Christ, since we shall all come right at last anyhow." Can this belief make men holy and happy? Some of you will answer, "It makes me happy for the present, and that is the most I care for." But does it make you *holy?* Does it beget true Christian self-denial and real benevolence? A faith and a practice which make you happy without being holy are but a poor thing. Indeed, it cannot fail of being utterly mischievous, because it lures and pleases without the least advance towards saving your soul. It only leaves you the more a slave of sin and Satan.

But you say, "It makes me so miserable to believe that any will be forever lost!"

What then? What if it does make you feel unhappy? It may make you unhappy to see your guilty friend sent to the penitentiary or the gallows now; but such a doom may be none the less deserved—none the less certain, because it hurts your feelings.

How can there be any other way of final happiness save through real holiness? The fountain of all happiness must lie in your own soul. If that is renewed to holiness and made unselfish, loving, forgiving, humble—then you will be happy of course,—but you cannot be happy without such a character.

Some of you may say, "I don't believe in the necessity of a change of heart."

Yes, *you do;* you are altogether mistaken in regard to the matter, if you suppose you don't believe in the necessity of a change of heart. There cannot be such a man in all Christendom—a man who does not know that by nature his heart is not right with God, yet that it must become right with God before he can enjoy God's presence in heaven. Is there one whose conscience does not testify that, before conversion, his heart is alienated from God? Do you not know that you are unlike God in spirit? and that you must be changed so as to become like God before you can enjoy Him? What! a sinner, knowing himself to be a sinner, believe he can be happy in God's presence without a radical moral change? Impossible! Every man knows that the sinner, out of sympathy with God, must be changed before he can enjoy God's presence and love. Every man, unchanged by God's grace, knows himself to be a sinner and not holy by nature.

A case in point to show the force of truth on even hardened hearts came lately to my knowledge. A Christian lady, being on a visit to one of the towns in Canada, was called on by a gentleman of high standing in society, but who had always lived a prayerless, ungodly life. A man of strong will and nerves, professedly a sceptic, he yet took the ground before this Christian lady that he was ready, as a means of becoming a Christian, to do anything that she should say. "Well, then," said she, "kneel down here, and cry out, 'God, be merciful to me, a sinner.'" "What!" replied he, "do this when I don't believe myself a sinner?" "You need not excuse yourself on that ground," said she, "for *you know you are a sinner.*" Having passed his word of honor to a lady, he could not draw back, and therefore kneeled and repeated the proposed words. Arising, he asked, "What next?" "Do so again, and say the same words." He raised the old objection, "I don't believe myself a sinner." She made the same answer as before, and a second time he repeated the words of that prayer. The same things were said—the same things done, the third time, and then, hardened as he was, his heart felt the force of those words, and he began to cry in earnest, "God, be merciful to me, a sinner!" His heart broke, and he prayed till mercy came!

So often, when men say they don't believe this and that, they *do believe it* so far as conviction is concerned. They *know the truth* respecting their own guilt.

But you plead, perhaps, this: I must attend to other duties first; my studies, or my business.

No, my friend; no other duties can come before this. This is the greatest duty and ought to be the first. Hear what the Saviour said on this very point. He said to one man, "Follow Me;" and he answered, "Lord, suffer me first to go and bury my father." This is a strong case, and is placed on record for our instruction because it is strong. It may seem to you very unnatural that Jesus would call any man away from a duty so obvious and so inborn in every human heart; yet what did He say? He gave no heed to this plea, but answered, "Let the dead bury their dead; but go thou and preach the kingdom of God." Not even the last rites of burial to the dead must be allowed to stand before obedience to Christ's call. No doubt Christ saw a disposition in this man to *plead* off, and therefore He saw the necessity of meeting it promptly. Suppose the man had said at first, "Yes, Lord, I am ready; my father lies unburied; but I am ready, if Thou callest me, to follow Thee even now;" it is at least supposable, if not probable, that Jesus would have answered, Yes; I will go with thee to that funeral. Let us lay the dead solemnly in their last bed, and then go to our preaching.

Another man replied to his call, saying, "Lord, I will follow Thee; but let me first go and bid them farewell which are at home in my house." To him, Jesus replied, "No man having put his hand to the plow and looking back, is fit for the kingdom of God." Thus Christ teaches that no duty can possibly come before this of giving up your heart to follow Him. You must make up your mind fully to this life-business, and really enter upon it. All things else are only an offence to God.

Do you say, I must study? You must first make up your mind to do all for Christ,—else study can be no acceptable duty. When Jesus says to you, "My son, give Me thy heart," He wants nothing else instead of your heart. He does not wish to be put off with some other duty than the very one He calls for. When He says, "Follow Me," He demands an explicit answer, whether you will or no, and He cannot accept anything evasive.